GREEK HISTORY AND BIBLICAL WISDOM

ROBERT FREIBERG

I0806042

STONE TOWER PRESS

Greek History and Biblical Wisdom

Stone Tower Press
7 Ellen Rd.
Middletown, RI 02842
stonetowerpress.com

ISBN: 979-8-9992313-5-2

Formatting and cover design by Amy Cole and Emily Olson, JPL Design Solutions.

Front cover graphic: King Leonidas and his 300 Spartans and a few allies, including the Thebans, standing against the invading Persians at the Battle of Thermopylae (480 BC). Alamy BWNB8B

Printed in the United States of America

TABLE OF CONTENTS

PREFACE

This book is a labor of love. I have found that while people are generally cordial when it comes to them listening about someone tell them about Jesus, they are not very enthusiastic about it. Jesus used over 50 different types of teaching methods, but the one I have found that is usually the most effective is the use of storytelling. Furthermore, people tend to be drawn in a little more if the story is true. However, to tell a story just to tell a story is a wasted endeavor—stories should have a point. It is a bit like what the ancient Greek slave Aesop did when he used animals to tell a story and then have a moral added that was related to the story and potentially made the listener a better person if he or she acted upon it.

This is the strategy I used as a Navy chaplain over 30 years ago. In Luke 5:10, Jesus had just performed a miracle by telling Peter to let down his nets and Peter in faith did what Jesus had asked him to with the result there was a great number of fish. It was after this that Jesus told Peter that from now on, Peter would be catching men. The word used for "catching" means that from now on, Peter would be "capturing alive," "bring under control" or "hold things in check" in the "catching" men for the glory of God. It is for this reason that I started these "Morning blessings."

While many in the commands in which I served were not Christians in the evangelical Protestant sense, many were raised with some kind of faith. So, by using something that is interesting and familiar, I was able to promote good order and discipline with those in the command. It was a way of presenting Jesus without any threat and a means to show that God's attributes and characteristics are all around us in how we deal with each other and treat one another—not to mention how glorious God is in this life.

First, I want to thank my co-laborer in the things of Christ for the past 48 years, my wife, Nancy. She, along with my friend Kurt Johnson, graciously went through my manuscript and made many, many corrections without telling me that I was a bonehead, which I always appreciate. Secondly, I want to thank my publisher, Tim Demy, who has been my friend and mentor in the Lord for the past 35 years. I also have Shane Blackmen to thank for giving me ideas and thoughts for many of the Scriptural applications contained in this project. Last, but not least, my brother in the flesh and in the Lord, Bruce my big brother, for his confidence in his little brother. We have come a long way since you accused me of stealing your Hopalong Cassidy lunchbox when we were kids.

Now, to the person I want most to dedicate this book, my brother-in-law, Mike Hendley. Mike and I have known each other for almost 50 years. When I first met you, you were the biggest sceptic when it came to things of faith. Now after all these years, you are faithful in attending your local church, committed in your weekly Bible studies, a father and husband who has been steadfast to all things that are good and righteous. One who has loved God, family and country all in that order. Oh, and that includes tennis, whatever that means for us non-tennis types.

My admiration for you is that for all these years, you have stood the test of time and have been faithful to those things which are right and pure in the eyes of God. As I have told you before, you are my Captain and someone I look up to during the crucible of time. You are one of the few men I knew who because of the influence and work of our practical cement mason fathers, could relate when I told stories of "making mud" and "carrying a hod" when we were younger men. Neither of us are flashy and exciting individuals, but salt of the earth men who understood the value of a simple, yet fulfilling life as fathers and husbands.

Oh, and the fact that we married sisters from the same family makes our lives shall we say… "interesting."

To the reader: may this book be used to bring you to a knowledge and love of God and ever closer to God. Enjoy! God bless.

Bob Freiberg, September 2025.

INTRODUCTION

Western civilization owes much to the Greeks—and so does Christianity. The New Testament was written in Greek and the world of early Christianity was influenced by the ideas, writings, philosophers, and history of ancient Greece, just as it was of the Roman Empire.

The teaching of the Bible are easily and readily illustrated from history. The purpose of the present volume is to look at ancient Greece and daily life in that society and culture. When we do so, we find many individuals and incidents that illustrate biblical thought and by application, relevance to our lives in the present. The stories in this work are presented in broad chronological order to assist in understanding some of the flow of Greek history. However, stories could have come from any empire, any nation, any person, or any era. The truths of the Bible are always valid and one can always find historical or contemporary events from any culture to illustrate those truths. "The grass withers, the flower fades, but the word of our God stands forever" (Isaiah 40:8).

II

THESEUS AND THE MINOTAUR

> "The Nephilim were on the earth in those days, and also afterward, when the sons of God came in to the daughters of men, and they bore children to them. Those were the mighty men who were of old, men of renown. Then the LORD saw that the wickedness of man was great on the earth, and that every intent of the thoughts of his heart was only evil continually. The LORD was sorry that He had made man on the earth, and He was grieved in His heart."
>
> GENESIS 6:4–6

One of the earliest stories of Greek mythology is a story of King Minos of Crete who prayed and asked Poseidon, god of the sea, for a sacrificial animal. Poseidon then presented the king with a beautiful white bull, but rather than sacrifice the beautiful animal, King Minos kept it for himself. In retribution, Poseidon cast a spell on Pasiphae, the wife of King Minos, causing her to fall in love with the animal. As a result of that union, the Minotaur was born, an animal which had the head and tail of a bull and the body of a man. Furthermore, the Minotaur had a desire for human flesh, so once every year, the king demanded seven young men and seven young women from the city of Athens to feed the Minotaur.

Because the Minotaur was dangerous and deadly, the king put him into a labyrinth from which he could never escape. Athens, a subservient city of the nation of Crete, raised up a hero named Theseus to kill the Minotaur. As Theseus descended into the labyrinth, he unrolled a ball of thread to find his way out of it once he had killed the beast. As he quietly moved through the darkness, he found the Minotaur asleep and killed him where he slept. Once successful in his mission, he followed the thread out of the labyrinth, where King Minos waited for the hero. During this confrontation, Theseus then killed the king, thus giving freedom to his native city of Athens.

If one visits the ancient site in Crete, there is found the ruins of a once great palace with multiple rooms with many nooks and crannies. This gives the possibility of the story being true. Likewise, there is an older story found in the Scriptures where spirit beings mated with humans, and in this case, the offspring produced some type of hybrid wicked spirit beings with human qualities. Only this time, the story is found in the pages of holy writ which means that it did happen. Some may say this is only one of a couple of interpretations concerning this passage. However, given the fact that there are other passages throughout Scripture that give further insight into this version of this interpretation, there is probably something to the origin of the wicked spirit beings. Unfortunately, this is too easily dismissed in Christian western culture. However, because it is in the Scriptures, we should heed the lesson which is "we wrestle not against flesh and blood, but power and principalities ... " (Ephesians 6:12). We should be wise and aware of spiritual warfare going on around us.

2

KING MIDAS AND THE MIDAS TOUCH

> "There is a grievous evil which I have seen under the sun: riches being hoarded by their owner to his hurt. When those riches were lost through a bad investment and he had fathered a son, then there was nothing to support him. As he had come naked from his mother's womb, so will he return as he came. He will take nothing from the fruit of his labor that he can carry in his hand."
>
> ECCLESIASTES 5:13–15

No doubt many of us have heard about King Midas of Phrygia (modern Turkey) of antiquity who was popular in Greek mythology. Historically speaking, there actually was a king named Midas who was the son of the famous King Gordius (the one who made a famous knot called "the Gordian Knot" that no person could undo). King Gordius's knot was finally undone after centuries of being on display when Alexander the Great came upon it years later, examined it for a few minutes, then took his sword and hacked it to pieces and told everyone he had just done the impossible by solving the mystery of the Gordian Knot ... but I digress from King Midas.

The story about King Midas has many facets, but in one Greek mythology version, Silenus the Satyr partied so hard that he passed out and was carried to King Midas's palace. Midas knowing him as a demi-god treated him with kindness, so Silenus in return granted the King one wish. Midas then asked if he could have the ability to turn any object he touched into gold. The wish was granted and eager to try out his new gift, Midas went out to his garden where all the flowers he touched instantly turned into gold. Overjoyed at this newfound gift, he went around touching everything, only to find out that this so-called gift was actually a curse and his eventual doom. Wanting the riches of this world, he discovered that even his food and drink were not immune to his touch and after a couple of days, he starved to death.

The saying "be careful what you wish for, you may get it," never rang truer. This, as well as the verses of the day, remind us that while we all crave personal wealth, it can create more trouble than what it is worth. As the second wisest person who ever lived (Jesus was the first), Solomon ponders his fate and his achievements before God. Due to his God-given wisdom, he eventually realizes how the pursuit of earthly things really has no meaning without the personal relationship and intimacy with God. What Solomon concluded after a lifetime of frustration was to "fear God and obey His commandments." However, the discovery today which is far better than gold and precious stones is the truth of knowing God personally by knowing His Son, Jesus Christ, which also happens to be the most valuable truth of all time.

3

THE THIRD TASK OF HERCULES

"But as he was discussing righteousness, self-control, and the judgment to come, Felix became frightened and said 'Go away for the present, and when I find time, I will summon you.'"

ACTS 24:25–26

In Greek mythology, one of the more interesting stories concerned a hero named Hercules. Hercules was driven mad by the queen of the gods Hera and in his fit killed his family. For punishment, King Eurystheus gave Hercules twelve labors to perform and if he were successful, he could earn his freedom back. Most of his tasks involved great feats of strength, but one of those tasks was quite delicate because he not only had to be patient, but diplomatic, which was not one of his strong traits.

The third of his tasks was to capture and bring back the "Ceryneian Hind." This was a stag which was sacred to the goddess Artemis, the goddess of the hunt. Hercules was a great hunter and could have easily hunted, shot, and killed the animal with a bow and arrow, but if he did that, he knew he would incur the wrath of Artemis. Instead, he followed and watched the animal for over a year and got to know its habits. By his patience and stealth, he planned to catch it without injuring it. Then, when the time was ready, he set a trap and captured the animal. He then carefully carried it to King Eurystheus and once the king saw it, Hercules released the stag, fulfilling this task.

In the story, Hercules could have done the easy thing, but he had other considerations which affected how he was to resolve his task. In this task, he learned another way of doing things. It must have stretched him as a person because it ran counter to how he usually did things, but through hard work, patience, and self-control, he was able to accomplish his goal.

Self-control in the Bible is a godly trait because when we have a desire to do something, we usually impulsively jump out and "scratch that itch." However, God gives us the ability to not do something that we desire and exercise self-control. This is important because in God's perfect will, He calls for us to be righteous, which means He has His standards but, because of sin, our first desire is to do our own thing. However, as we work on our self-control through discipline, we can conform ourselves to the will of God. The good return on doing something God's way is that we can enjoy the blessings of God Himself as He showers us with His love and affection. So, learn the lesson from Hercules and exercise some self-control to keep from sinning today.

4

ACHILLES HAS A HISSY FIT

"Beloved, do not avenge yourselves, but rather give place to wrath, for it is written, 'Vengeance is Mine, I will repay,' says the Lord."

ROMANS 12:19

In Homer's *Iliad,* the story deals with the ten-year long war between the Greeks and the Trojans. As the story opens, it describes the conflict between the greatest warrior of the Greeks, Achilles, with the leader of the Greek confederation, King Agamemnon. The Greeks had just sacked a city and were dispersing the booty of money and prisoners. As a result of his actions, Achilles's valor won the admiration and respect of his fellow soldiers, so he was given the beautiful captive woman Briseis, the greatest treasure in the city, as a war trophy. However, when the time came for Achilles to claim his rightful prize, Agamemnon as the leader stepped in and took the slave girl for himself.

Suffering injustice, this event proved to be the ultimate undoing of Achilles. The rest of the *Iliad* tells the story of Achilles' moral outrage resulting from this incident and how it changes him because of this inequality. He first expresses his anger. Next, he builds up his case and tells everyone around him of the injustices he has suffered at the hands of a bad leader. Finally, he pouts and then leaves the battle and all his friends behind to fend for themselves without his leadership. Feeling his loss, his best friend Patroklos tries to rally the troops without Achilles but is instead killed in battle. Upon hearing of the loss of his friend, the grieving Achilles now wants revenge and ends up in a killing frenzy followed by his moral and character decline. He is last shown killing the Trojan Prince Hector and publicly defiling his corpse to the amazement and shame of everyone. Eventually he incurs the wrath of the gods and with their help, the least warrior of all, Paris, Hector's younger brother, kills Achilles.

Who among us has never had an injustice done toward us? In the darkest recesses of our hearts, we scheme, and work plans to get our vengeance from those who did us wrong. Unfortunately, our bitterness affects others and eventually it taints how we view life and others. We become skeptics and get cynical about everything. It doesn't need to be this way. There is another way and that is to understand injustice happens to all of us. It is a way for God to demonstrate His way is better. While we want to destroy and get our revenge, God says, "Let it go!" God will someday repay the person's injustice done to you; so we don't have to do it. No one escapes God. In the meantime, we learn forgiveness from God and it frees us from the bonds of our anger. We also get to keep our integrity in the long run ... but how to start? Reading God's Word is a good start and from there, try some alone time with the Lord in prayer. It takes the bite out of injustice! I guarantee it!

5

THE LEGACY OF THE GREEK CITY-STATE OF THEBES

"But God, being rich in mercy, because of His great love with which He loved us, even when we were dead in our transgressions, made us alive together with Christ (by grace you have been saved), and raised us up with Him, and seated us with Him in the heavenly places in Christ Jesus."

EPHESIANS 2:4–6

Ancient Thebes in Greece was the pinnacle of all things Greek for over a thousand years. It was ground zero for Greek literature, drama and culture. It was here where most of Greek mythology and stories of their origins started, such as the adventures of Hercules, along with the many gods and goddesses of antiquity. It was the city of Thebes where many of the plays by Euripides were set, giving an air of authenticity to his tragic plays. For over a millennium it was the place where the rich and famous monuments were built and extolled the virtue of all that the human spirit could capture.

Thebes rivaled the might and wisdom of ancient Athens and was the nation that humbled Sparta. However, in 335 BC, Alexander the Great, as the new king of Macedonia, sent a delegate to Thebes to discuss terms of surrender. Alexander was a new king and had to establish himself as the leader of all Greeks and Thebes was the place to make this happen. However, the Theban council held captive the Macedonia delegation and in retaliation, Alexander brought the full might of his army and destroyed the city of Thebes. He leveled the city and its 1,000-year history with its monuments, killed all its fighting age men, sold the children and women into slavery and after that Thebes never did recover its pre-eminence in the Greek world. Much of what was Thebes was lost for all time after Alexander.

It was one of the times in history when one civilization destroyed another. In the ancient world, that is how they did warfare. In stark contrast however, despite having weapons which have the capability to destroy whole civilizations, western civilization for the past 2,000 years has held off doing that to nations. The reason is because of our two-thousand-year history of embracing Christianity. However, as we become further removed from the constraints of morality based on the nature and character of God, this will change. The reason for this is found in the verses of the day. As we love God through Christ, it changes us from the inside out. It is the inner man which makes moral decisions, and it is that inner relationship which controls how we behave and act.

If one were to analyze the New Testament book of Ephesians, the first three chapters deal with interrogative truth about the nature and character of God, while the last couple of chapters are written in the imperative tense. In other words, after Paul wrote about the nature and character of God, then he told us how we should use that truth to conform ourselves to the nature and image of God Himself. It is by knowing and understanding God, that we can become more Christ-like and unlike Alexander with the city state of Thebes, learn to be more forgiving and gracious.

6

ODYSSEUS VERSUS ORPHEUS

> "The angel of the LORD encamps around those who fear Him And rescues them. O taste and see that the LORD is good; How blessed is the man who takes refuge in Him!"
>
> PSALM 34:7–8

In the ancient world of Greek myths, there is a story about a group of muses called "The Sirens." These were a group of woman-like creatures who inhabited an island and sang songs from the top of cliffs to ships passing by. As sailors heard the magical songs, they would be driven mad, only to have their ships destroyed on the rocks near the island, causing all the men to drown. It was a dangerous part of the world, and no man could resist its melody once it was heard. To go near this island was certain death.

There were only two instances in ancient literature where men were able to go near the island and live. One was the story of Odysseus on his way home with his men when he went by the island. He cleverly stopped up the ears of his men with wax to prevent them from hearing the song of the Sirens. However, for his part he chained himself to the mast of the ship to hear their songs because he wanted to be tempted and hear them, but his chains prevented him from jumping into the water to certain death. For doing this, the passage in the *Odyssey* tells how he was tormented beyond reason. The songs brought distress and anguish to Odysseus, but he lived through it.

The second story is found from the journey of Jason and the Argonauts in their search for the Golden Fleece. In this story, a master musician who played the harp by the name of Orpheus was part of the crew. It was said that his music was so impressive that when he played his lyre, even the gods would stop and listen.

This time, instead of preventing themselves from hearing the dangerous melody of the sirens, Jason told the crew to listen to Orpheus play as they went by the island. As the sweet music of Orpheus played while the crew rowed, it drowned out the dangerous tunes of the wicked Sirens. So, as Orpheus played his sweet melodies, the men of the ship never paid any attention to the outside songs and thus, passed the dangerous island in complete safety and it is this analogy that we need to focus on today. We as believers have choices in life. As Christians who possess the joy and sweetness of Christ, we can either tie ourselves to the mast of a ship and long for the song of the sinful, wicked world and be tormented all our lives, or seek after the pureness of what the Lord has to offer us. As the crew focused on the harmony, melody and rhythm of Orpheus's compositions, the crew was satisfied, safe, and never distracted. The choice of destruction or prosperity is obvious. Listening to the sweet song of salvation with Jesus is the best choice.

7

ONLY FOR WINNERS

"Let love of the brethren continue. Do not neglect to show hospitality to strangers, for by this some have entertained angels without knowing it."

HEBREWS 13:1–2

One of the themes in ancient Greek mythology is the idea of the gods, who normally stayed home on Mt Olympus, walked among humans. A good example of this is found in Acts 14 when Paul and Barnabas were mistaken for Zeus and Hermes by the locals. However, in Greek mythology there is another, darker side which may have had a little bit of truth in it and that is the idea that the gods came down and had sexual relations with humans. For instance, Hercules is the son of Zeus in this manner, as well as Helen and Polydeuces were offspring from the union of their mother queen Ledo and Zeus, in the form of a swan. These stories, often explained as mythology, have a big part in many cultures around the world to this day. Actually, it's not much of a stretch to believe these stories, given we even have an example in the Bible.

We find in Genesis 6, that the "sons of God" (a euphemism for demons), saw that the "daughters of men" were beautiful and had sexual relations with them. The union of these two entities produced offspring named in the Bible as Rephaim, Anakim, and Amim. Beings who lived in the area in what is now modern Jordan during the time of Moses as described in the book of Deuteronomy. While the correct interpretation of Genesis 6 is debated among scholars, the idea that spirit beings came down and mingled with humans is a topic found in both secular and Biblical readings. Whether with malicious intent or not, the idea of both good angels and bad angels or demons coming to earth and interacting with humans is something consistent throughout the Scriptures. This idea is often not discussed in western Christian circles because of our aversion to "anything superstitious" as found in other cultures. However, it is something perhaps all Bible reading Christians should spend a little more time studying, so they are a little more tuned to the nature of the spiritual world around us. Who knows, perhaps we all have had dealings with angels somewhere or somehow?

The biggest proof of this being a distinct likelihood is an event in history which is undeniable. It is the incontrovertible fact that God Himself decided to come down to earth as a human child. What this did was to prove to the world that God was real and could relate to humanity. Christ Himself said "He who has seen me, has seen the Father" (John 14:9). It also showed that God was not some invisible abstract concept in the sky somewhere, but that He was real and had substance and understood our inner thoughts and needs. Most of all though, it showed His great love for us by meeting the need to pay the price of our sin, so that we could have not only eternal life, but also forgiveness. In His humanity, He felt and did everything we do, except sin. In his humanity, He is still fully God.

8

DEMOCRATIC VOTES

"He was in the world, and the world was made through Him, and the world did not know Him. He came to His own, and those who were His own did not receive Him. But as many as received Him, to them He gave the right to become children of God, even to those who believe in His name, who were born, not of blood nor of the will of the flesh nor of the will of man, but of God."

JOHN 1:10–13

Since the times of ancient Egypt, broken pottery bits have been used on which to write things. The smooth surface of a piece of pottery was an easy medium to write or scratch notes on and once a message was conveyed, the pottery shard or ostraca was discarded, only to be found by some excited archaeologist centuries later. Fortunately for us, many of these ostraca were not destroyed and what was written on them in the form of words or marks gives us in the contemporary world a light into the workings of the ancient world.

For instance, a hoard of used ostraca was found by archaeologists digging in Athens in 1960 revealed the results of a vote taken by Greeks around 471 BC. The vote in this case was the banishment for ten years of a man whom others did not like or with whom they did not agree. In the Greek system of democracy, all rights for some people were suspended if there was a vote to get rid of an individual—hence the process called "ostracized." It didn't matter what the people had agreed on for individual rights or liberty because on certain occasions these rights were suspended, and a vote was taken to banish a person from the state. If the government leaders voted in a majority, then that person had to leave the city for ten years.

The point of today's reflection is to show how the human majority who rule can be wrong about decisions. A good example from the Bible is the "ostracizing" of the Lord Jesus before the Jewish leaders known as "the Sanhedrin." Of course, it was their decision to condemn Jesus despite all His miracles and proofs that He was the Messiah. So much for the wisdom of human leadership and the use of democracy within a body. There is a responsibility before God and man to do what is right and of course many in times past and present in leadership positions have made terrible decisions which affect others. Fortunately for us, Jesus rose from the dead and disproved the folly of the ruling voting body.

9

DRACO AND DEMOCRACY

"Therefore there is now no condemnation for those who are in Christ Jesus. For the law of the Spirit of life in Christ Jesus has set you free from the law of sin and of death. For what the Law could not do, weak as it was through the flesh, God did: sending His own Son in the likeness of sinful flesh and as an offering for sin, He condemned sin in the flesh, so that the requirement of the Law might be fulfilled in us, who do not walk according to the flesh but according to the Spirit."

ROMANS 8:1–4

The Greek statesman Draco (d. 600 BC) was an ancient Greek lawgiver who gave the first constitution to the ancient Athenians. Before Draco, the city-state was run by leaders known as "Archons," who were rich elites who ruled the city of Athens. They ruled in such a corrupt manner that the people in the city had to take drastic measures to ensure safety. As with what usually happens in this kind of a situation, the common people reacted and threw the Archons out of power. From this event a man named Draco came into power and punished the rich as well as the lower classes. As a result, he instituted harsh measures into the law and listed numerous capital offenses, such as having a man killed if he stole a cabbage. The penalty for disobedience to the law was terrible, (hence the term " Draconian," meaning "severe" in relation to laws). Severe and excessive measures in the law were enacted to preserve the peace.

We know of these laws because they were inscribed in wood and placed in the agora, or marketplace for all to see. The tablets were set on a pyramid and displayed for all to see, so all could understand what the law said. Even though the laws were meant for everyone, it soon became apparent that the upper class wielded more power and to keep that power, enforced the laws only against the poor in such a way which wrecked the idea of equal justice. So, eventually Draco was banished, and a new lawgiver named Solon came to prominence. What seemed like a good idea only lasted a short time.

History is full of stories of cultures that had problems with one group of people regarding another group. Unfairness and inequity are a fact of life due to the sinfulness of humanity. What is right in one person's eyes might be a grievance to another. Sometimes a short-term solution simply adds to the problem. One thing that is true in our verses of the day is when God handles a problem, it always stays solved. Take for instance, He has declared that *all* of humanity are sinful and compared to His holiness and righteousness have offended Him (after all, He is God). This is a decree that shows God sets the standard of what is good and bad. There is no middle ground and despite what the best human ethics are, He settles the question and sets the gold standard for righteousness. Everyone is guilty and not one person deserves to live. However, and unlike Draco, God does not leave the law there but provides a way of redemption out of that pit, which is faith in the payment for sin, namely, the death on the cross, burial and resurrection of Christ. The penalty for sin is death, but the gift of God is eternal life.

10

SOLON AND REPUBLICANISM

"That which has been that which will be, and that which has been done is that which will be done. So, there is nothing new under the sun. Is there anything of which one might say, 'See this, it is new'? Already it has existed for ages which were before us."

ECCLESIASTES 1:9–10

Solon (d. 560 BC) was an ancient Greek philosopher, poet, politician and warrior known for his many reforms in the political arena of democracy. Little remains of his original writings, but we know a lot about his thoughts and deeds due to his being quoted by many people who came after him. It was his life and ideas about government that our Founding Fathers turned to when trying to determine what type of government we should have here in the United States. He was one of the few in antiquity who had figured out a workable way to make a society of both rich and poor work side by side harmoniously for the common good in which both classes would benefit in peace.

Ancient Athens was first ruled by nine *archons* who were wealthy landowners who held all the power in the city. The upper class (the *ekklesia*) were the only ones allowed to vote and discuss policy and laws. This was carried out on the "Areopagus," the same place where centuries later the apostle Paul debated about Christ as recorded in Acts 17:22. In Solon's era the lower class (*thetes*) were left out, until Solon changed the Athenian constitution to allow them to participate in the *ekklesia*. Further, there was a court (the *heliaia*) made up of both rich and poor and its purpose was to adjudicate and hold accountable all elected officials. It was the beginning of representative form of government which later became known as "republicanism."

The problems between the rich and poor have been around since biblical times, and as a result, this tension and divide has caused civilizations to come and go. Even Solomon saw that in his era as recorded in the verses of the day. In modern times, both the American and French Revolutions changed forms of government, but the one that stuck and is still in place is the American republic. The difference is that the American Revolution never sought to do away with the existing government, while hanging onto its biblical Christian roots. We are a democratic republic, much like what Solon had envisaged, but while his model only lasted a short while, ours has lasted because there is one factor that he never thought of and that is a belief in a sovereign God who rules in the hearts and minds of people regenerated by the Spirit of Christ. It is this moral truth that historically binds us not only together as a people but joins us together in soul and spirit with a God of moral absolutes and truth. While the form of government is important and has allowed us to flourish, it is the sovereign love of God who we believe in that is the real key to our successful form of government.

11

AESOP'S FABLES

"Offer the sacrifices of righteousness, And trust in the LORD. Many are saying, 'Who will show us any good?' Lift the light of Your countenance upon us, O LORD! You have put gladness in my heart, more than when their grain and new wine abound."

PSALM 4:5–7

Aesop was a Greek slave who lived in the 6th century BC. He was a prolific writer of proverbs and fables. He is mentioned often in antiquity and is quoted by Aristotle, Plutarch, and many others. People have even written about where he was from and the name of the person who owned him as a slave. Many ancient sources even give the years in which he was born and died. However, modern "scholarship" leads us to believe he never existed and was fabricated ... at least according to the leading Aesop scholar as recently as the 1960s. Fortunately, this is a reflection about the merits of what is taught through these fables, instead of the credibility of modern scholarship.

However, without debating the merits of the scholars, we do have some fables that are not only entertaining but give an important moral about life. One favorite fable was "The Lion and the Mouse." It's a tale about the king of the beasts who was resting one day and a small mouse darted across the great lion's nose. Using his big paw, he trapped the mouse and told him he was going to crush him because he disturbed his sleep. The quick-thinking mouse told the lion that if he let him go, then later, he would always be there to help the lion. The lion laughed at the tiny mouse's offer, snickered once more and let him go.

Later, the lion was walking in the forest, and a great net pinned him to the ground. No matter how much he struggled, he couldn't get free. In desperation he gave up and it was at that moment the mouse came up and started gnawing at the ropes. He did that until the lion was able to break free. The moral of the story can be grasped by reflecting on the verses of the day. We are like the mouse who remains loyal to the lion, but in this case, it is the lion who always guides and protects us. We can offer our friendship and loyalty, but it is God who gives the increase in all things. He, like the lion who laughed at the offering of the mouse, is a great God who does not need anything from us but only asks of us to offer a sacrifice of righteousness. Of course, God does not have any weaknesses like the lion, but He offers us many promises for our faithfulness to Him. In return, the Lion of Judah will always watch and protect us in all things.

12

ANDROCLES AND THE LION

"I will give You thanks with all my heart; I will sing praises to You before the gods. I will bow down toward Your holy temple and give thanks to Your name for Your lovingkindness and Your truth; For You have magnified Your word according to all Your name. On the day I called, you answered me; you made me bold with strength in my soul."

PSALM 138:1–3

For those of us who are older, we grew up with many stories from *Aesop's Fables* (also known as *Aesopica*). One of my favorite stories was called "Androcles and the Lion." It is a story which takes place in ancient Greece about a slave boy who escapes his cruel master, only to be found in the woods later facing a wild, raging lion. However, as the lion comes closer, the boy finds the lion in great pain because it has a thorn stuck in his mighty paw. The boy nervously pulls out the thorn and to his relief, the lion prances away from him. The boy is later caught and for punishment he is thrown into a pit, where a man-eating lion is waiting to kill and eat him. Yet when he goes into the pit, the lion recognizes him as the one who pulled out the thorn in his paw and instead of killing the slave boy, he goes up to him and licks him. The story ends with the boy and the lion being freed and they lived happily ever after.

In modern times, this story was adapted by the playwright George Bernard Shaw in 1912 and made into a Broadway play. However, the atheist Shaw took the theme and story and made it into a satire on religion. The slave boy became a Christian in ancient Rome, and it was used as a backdrop where Androcles was thrown into the coliseum because he was a Christian for refusing to pay homage to the state religion of Caesar worship. Androcles and his fellow believers skillfully describe to the captain of the Emperor's Guard how foolish was the organized religion of the Romans compared to the goodness of Christianity. The bottom line was that the Christians were sold out to God at all costs, and they were willing to die for their belief in the One True God.

Although the gospel of Jesus Christ is never mentioned in the story, it nonetheless shows how God can be glorified in the arts, literature and music. David understood this and he wrote many Psalms to testify of the wonder and glory of our Lord through the media of poetry and music. In his praise, he finds the right words and, accompanied by music, he not only describes God and His marvelous works, but also expresses his wonder and joy while singing praises to Him. It is how our God-given gifts and emotions should be used to appreciate and revel in fellowship with God while we commune with Him. As a result of knowing this truth, may you find the wonder of God today. May you also use your creative ability to find ways using the performing arts to extol the God we love.

13

MILO OF CROTON

"For with You is the fountain of life; In Your light we see light. O continue Your lovingkindness to those who know You, And Your righteousness to the upright in heart. Let not the foot of pride come upon me and not let the hand of the wicked drive me away."

PSALM 36:9–11

Occasionally, we come across a person who is larger than life. You know them, they are the ones who enter a room, and they immediately become the center and focus of attention. One such man was Milo of Croton. Some of what we know of him is probably fiction, but we do know he was a real man who lived in ancient Greece. Early in his life it is said that Milo saw a calf and put the calf on his shoulders until he was tired. He continued this exercise every day as he and the calf got bigger and heavier and so eventually, he got used to lifting large animals. Such was how he grew strong. It is said he saved the life of Pythagoras (you know, the person credited with the "Pythagorean Theorem") and was a tremendous athlete by winning ancient Greek games at the Olympic, Isthmian and Nemean contests. Known for his strength, he was also very proud and loved to show off by demonstrating to others his various feats of strength. Unfortunately for him, he did this into his 40's when his strength started to diminish.

One day, when he was walking through a forest, he saw a tree stump with a wedge in the middle of it. As a matter of personal pride, he thought he could split the tree stump in half with his bare hands. When he attempted it, the wedge popped out and the tree stump snapped back trapping his hands. He was too proud to call for help and try as he may, his strength failed him, and he grew weaker and weaker by the hour. He finally died and his carcass was fodder for the wild beasts. Such was the gruesome end of a man who exhibited a lot of pride.

One could say he was a self-made man and through hard work, did it himself. However, in the verse of the day, the Psalmist knows and understands that everything he is and learns comes from God. While accomplishments will bring personal pride, it is God who works in us and through us to achieve great things. Be careful about thinking that what you have done in this life is your own doing because like Milo, your pride can be your own undoing. The lesson is if you rely on yourself 100% of the time, you will fail. The principle is like the children of Israel when they left Egypt. They were given untold riches by their captives only so they could in turn give the precious stones back to God while they later built the tabernacle for His glory. So, if you have been successful in something, great! But remember God has allowed you to flourish, so make sure to give back to Him the credit.

14

HERACLITUS AND THE LOGOS

> "In the beginning was the Word, and the Word was with God, and the Word was God."
>
> JOHN 1:1

In the 6th century BC, there lived a man named Heraclitus. He wrote only one book that we are aware of and only fragments of that book survive today in quotations of other authors. It was a book written on cosmology, and his belief that everything in the universe was created by fire, and it formed the basis of order in the universe. Furthermore, he believed that everything in the universe had balance and order and that order had a name: the *logos.*

It was the *logos* that people needed to understand, so they could appreciate the orderliness of all things naturally and supernaturally. The ocean had water, and water sustains life for those creatures who live in it but is dangerous for those traveling on top of it during storms. Without the Logos, we would not understand good without the bad. The manifestation of the *logos* helps us to live in social harmony and know that there is a connection between all things and when something happens, there is an inner deep-seeded understanding of the order.

Reading about Heraclitus and his view of the *logos* also gives us insight into the work of the Holy Spirit in the world inside and around us. No doubt it is with this understanding that the Apostle John wrote that Jesus was the *Logos* (*word*) which was with God and was God. At the end of the first century, everyone knew and understood the philosophical and spiritual meaning of the *Logos* and instead of it being an abstract term, it had its embodiment in the person of Jesus Christ. It is He who helps us to understand the world around us, mainly because it was He who created it and by His nature holds all things together (Colossians 1:15–17). All the laws of physics and of the spiritual world have their being in Him. Yet, He loved us enough to die on the cross for our sins. May this truth ring in your hearts today as we praise His Name!

15

THEMISTOCLES SAVES THE DAY!

> "Be diligent to present yourself approved to God as a workman who does not need to be ashamed, accurately handling the word of truth. But avoid worldly and empty chatter, for it will lead to further ungodliness ... "
>
> 2 TIMOTHY 2:15–16

Themistocles (d. 459 BC) was an Athenian general and politician. He was very popular with the common people of Athens and was constantly in trouble with the political leaders known as "The Archons." It was his skill as a leader that convinced the leaders and the people of Athens to prepare for war against the Persians before the Persians were a threat to the city-state. Having convinced the Athenians to build over 200 triremes (a three-tiered galley ship), they were instrumental in the Athenian defeat of the Persians at the Battle of Salamis (480 BC).

It was here that the genius of Themistocles was revealed. Although Athens had the military equipment and men, they were still outnumbered and outgunned, but it was Themistocles once again who led to the eventual defeat of the Persians (led by king Xerxes, Esther's eventual husband as we read in the book of Esther). Knowing that the Persians had larger ships that couldn't maneuver in the narrow Strait of Salamis, Themistocles laid a trap for the Persians. To get the enemy to go into the strait, Themistocles had to pretend to be a traitor to the Persian general and convince the enemy the best course of action against the Athenians was to fight them there at the strait. Once they fell for the subterfuge, the smaller and more navigable ships of the Athenian navy picked off the larger ships and won the day.

In today's world one danger to our way of life is the malicious use of artificial intelligence (AI) that is used to trick us with false images and other things. Used right, AI could benefit humanity, but it's already being used for subterfuge and deceit of many because it is so close to the real thing that people are being tricked by it. Like the Persian general, many are being deceived by it. So, what is the best defense against such things? Well, the first thing is to realize that it cannot do anything that its human programmers don't put in the program. Programmers creating deceit reject the moral and ethical aspect of AI. Secondly, don't believe everything you see and read on public media. Be an educated consumer. The next thing is to go to a good church that teaches and preaches God's truth from the Word of God and helps you have a Christian worldview. Through this, you will learn truth through the Holy Spirit, which brings discernment to be wise. Wisdom brings the ability to distinguish that which is true from that which is false. Sure, Christians can be fooled, however, just the idea knowing that something could be false puts one on guard and that is a good start. So, be diligent and wise when handling the Word of God and the Lord will give you discernment in this deceptive world controlled by Satan and his demons. Be vigilant in the Lord!

16

THEMISTOCLES THE WISE!

"But flee from these things, you man of God, and pursue righteousness, godliness, faith, love, perseverance, and gentleness. Fight the good fight of faith; take hold of the eternal life to which you were called, and you made the good confession in the presence of many witnesses."

1 TIMOTHY 6:11–13

After winning the Battle of Salamis in 480 BC, the Athenians had to rebuild their city which was destroyed by the invading Persians. Their main defense had been two walls which went from the city to the harbor and that was destroyed in the war. After the war, the city states of Greece held a council and decided that each city was to be equal, so they decided that no defenses would be built around each respective city. The war was over, and the combined might of Greece defeated the mighty power of King Xerxes of Persia or, so it was said.

Athens for its part disagreed with the rest of the Greeks. After all, they had pretty much defeated the Persians by themselves and their leader Themistocles knew this was a ruse by the other Greek city-states for a potential takeover later, especially Sparta. What Sparta couldn't take by force they would take by subterfuge. So, while negotiating with the others, Themistocles secretly told the folks back in Athens to rebuild the defensive wall. He delayed the Spartan embassy to Athens by feigning sickness and doing all he could to delay their delegation overseeing the dismantling of any future Athenian defenses. Once the wall was built, he knew no one would try to overtake Athens again. Feeling safe once again after the rebuilding of the walls, he let the Spartan delegation in, and one can only imagine their indignation having been lied to by him. For the Athenians part, Themistocles knew the Spartans were an aggressive warrior caste and would use their access for their advantage sometime in the future.

We live in a fallen world of filled with sin. It is not wrong to be strong, but strength should never be used to oppress others. When Israel was walking by faith with God, they were strong, and no one messed with them. It was when they had backslidden that they were picked apart by foreign enemies. Such is the way with nations, but in stark contrast is the verse of the day which tells us that we are to be meek. Meek is a unique word because it means "power under control." In other words, one has the power to be strong physically but chooses not to use it. In the context of the passage, we as believers should choose to seek after things such as righteousness, meekness, love, and gentleness because they are things which enable us to be intimate with God. Embracing these things allow us to see a different kind of strength from God's point of view. Besides, if one trusts God, we have the strongest force in the world to protect us. Eternity with Christ outlasts any nation, and it is far better investment for those of us who seek to please God.

17

PHEIDIAS AND THE PARTHENON

> "When they came to the place called The Skull, there they crucified Him and the criminals, one on the right and the other on the left. But Jesus was saying, 'Father, forgive them; for they do not know what they are doing.'"
>
> LUKE 23:33–34

We have all heard of Michelangelo, Bernini, Donatello, and even Leonardo di Vinci as the best artists of all time. Their works have inspired others and people have studied their paintings to the "nth" degree. On the other hand, there is a man in antiquity who everyone knew during his lifetime, but whose name is unknown to many today. Some of his works are still around for us to enjoy and have stood the test of time for its detail, precision of nature and realism. In fact, one of his works was included in the seven wonders of the ancient world and was the inspiration behind the artist who designed the Lincoln Memorial. He was a man noted not only for his talent and brilliance, but also for his ability to forgive others despite severe persecution for his talent

Phidias or Pheidias (480–430 BC), was a Greek painter, architect, and sculptor. He was the talent behind the famous Elgin marbles friezes and pediment of the ancient Parthenon. He also created out of ivory and gold, a three-story high statue of "Athena Parthenos" which the Parthenon was built around. It took him eight years to oversee the construction and when he was finished, his fame spread throughout the ancient world. However, a group of jealous artists accused him of pilfering the gold used in the statue and by using trumped up charges against him, they were able to have him banished for a time. Eventually, he forgave those who falsely accused him (one account said he even proved his innocence) and went back to work by creating the famous statue of Zeus which, when finished, was considered a wonder of the world.

The story of Phidias is quite extraordinary. Not that he was the best artist in the world, but that he was able to forgive those who wronged him. This is a test of one's character and his story should inspire all of us to possess this godly trait. Forgiveness is a powerful act that can be even stronger than love—especially when one remembers the sin of a person against another. It is in this light that we should always remember how God forgave us through Christ's sacrifice in payment for our sins against Him. Phidias was able to achieve his greatest glory once he put his forgiveness behind him. In the same way, once we discover the freeing feeling of God's forgiveness, we are empowered to do good things for God. Protestant reformer Martin Luther used this freedom to proclaim God's love and look how he changed the world. We, who are just ordinary people, can be used by God for extraordinary things once we discover the truth of forgiveness. So, what are you waiting for? Don't you have a three-story statue to create?

18

DEIOCES THE MEDE

"They entered the covenant to seek the LORD God of their fathers with all their heart and soul; and whoever would not seek the LORD God of Israel should be put to death, whether small or great, man or woman. Moreover, they made an oath to the LORD with a loud voice, with shouting, with trumpets and with horns. All Judah rejoiced concerning the oath, for they had sworn with their whole heart and had sought Him earnestly, and He let them find Him. So the LORD gave them rest on every side."

2 CHRONICLES 15:12–15

Much of what we know about Persian (Iranian) early history comes from the ancient Greek historian Herodotus (d. 425 BC). It was he who expounded on who the class of priests/scientists known as the magi and gave Western civilization clarity on who they were and why they were important. He was also the source for telling us about many of the tribes of modern Iran which are mentioned in the Bible. For instance, his narrative, although sometimes faulty, told those in the western nations about the small kingdom of the Medes. This is important because it was the Medes who broke up the ancient kingdom of Assyria, which if you know your Bible history, were the ones who conquered and destroyed the northern kingdom of Israel in 722 BC.

According to Herodotus, the Medes started out as a modest group of villagers. The villages were given over to anarchy and injustice until a man arose named Deioces, who was renowned for his wisdom in dispensing justice. The more he judged, the more popular he got until one day he told them he wanted buildings, and a city built to his specifications. The people refused, so he stopped hearing cases from the people. Life fell into chaos once again, so the people then begged him to start judging them again. So, while he judged them, they built a city with great walls and beautiful courtyards with splendid palaces. They eventually made him king and after his death his son was the one who threw off the Assyrian yoke. This was the city of Ecbatana, the capital of the ancient Medes. Deioces ruled over them for 53 years.

The point of today's reflection is while the Greek historian Herodotus noted that Assyria was conquering foreign lands, they ignored the threat right under their nose. In God's providential plan, the Medes had 50 years of peace to consolidate their power base. Meaning that while the Medo-Babylonian alliance was being built up against Assyria, it gave Judah rest for a short time. In the verses of the day, when the people of God praised and worshipped God, He gave them peace and rest on every side. In a modern application, our world situation with China and Russia is precarious and the winds of war are visible. With this possibility, we as a nation, which are made up of individual believers, need to come to God and pray for His peace. For even if we had a Deioces, it doesn't matter. God in His sovereignty is the One who gives and takes away peace for His purposes. May we pray for His grace in peace during our perilous times.

19

HERODOTUS THE HISTORIAN

"Likewise, I want women to adorn themselves with proper clothing, modestly and discreetly, not with braided hair and gold or pearls or costly garments, but rather by means of good works, as is proper for women making a claim to godliness."

1 TIMOTHY 2:9–10

Today's reflection comes from the pages of the Greek historian Herodotus (d. 425 BC). Herodotus was a resident of Halicarnassus (modern Bodrum, Turkey) which sat on the western edge of the Persian empire and wrote about the customs and cultures of ancient Babylon, Assyria and Persia. For years his work, *Histories* was the most read source outside of the Bible for those living in the Western world for learning about the cultures of the ancient world. It is one of those stories which we now focus.

In Book 1.199, Herodotus writes there was a custom in ancient Babylon to appease the goddess of love known as Mylitta (which he says is the Babylonian name for Aphrodite), where each young maiden from every family, whether rich or poor, had to participate in a "shameful" (Herodotus's word, not mine) ritual. When the maiden was of age, each young woman had to go to a specific temple site and put on special garments and sit in a circle where young men would come by and inspect the young women. At the man's choosing, the man would take a silver coin and throw it in a maiden's lap who he had elected and say, "the goddess Mylitta prosper thee." Once selected, the young woman, by law had to go with that young man for a conjugal visit. Once consummated, the young woman had fulfilled her sacred duty to the nation. It sounds simple, but the problem arose when none of the young maidens were ever chosen due to being "ugly" (Herodotus's word, not mine). In fact, some young maidens were not so young because they stayed in this ritual for 3 to 4 years and couldn't go home until their obligation was fulfilled.

While we may consider this a barbaric practice, we have much of the same thing going on in our use of social media. Of course, young teen and pre-teen girls are most vulnerable to the slights of others found in the video screens of cell phones. Sometimes these crushing missives by insensitive miscreants can become the cause of suicide. A tragic thing indeed! That is why the Word of God is needed even more today than ever. In today's verses, God reveals what is important to a young woman to instill a sense of self-worth to get over the insecurity of superficial beauty. It is not the outward appearance which should matter to a young woman, but a call for godly character which is precious in the sight of God. To do this I call upon all fathers who have young daughters to spend time with them and love them as Christ loved the church. Teach them to be godly and their true beauty will last beyond the years of youth and extend well into golden years, for they will have continual praise from all due to her radiant countenance which comes from the Lord Himself! Every girl needs to know that she is important and loved by God.

20

A CASE OF ANCIENT PTSD

> "But as for me, I trust in You, O LORD, I say, 'You are my God.' My times are in Your hand; Deliver me from the hand of my enemies and from those who persecute me. Make Your face to shine upon Your servant; Save me in Your lovingkindness. Let me not be put to shame, O LORD, for I call upon You."
>
> PSALM 31:14–17

Herodotus was a Greek writer (d. 425 BC) who explains in his *Histories* (6.117) about a warrior while fighting, suddenly lost his eyesight and his blindness continued for the rest of his life. He writes:

> In this fight at Marathon there were slain of the Barbarians about six thousand four hundred men, and of the Athenians a hundred and ninety and two. Such was the number which fell on both sides; and it happened also that a marvel occurred there of this kind:— an Athenian, Epizelus the son of Cuphagoras, while fighting in the close combat and proving himself a good man, was deprived of the sight of his eyes, neither having received a blow in any part of his body nor having been hit with a missile, and for the rest of his life from this time he continued to be blind ...

Epizelos was affected mentally and emotionally by what he was going through as a soldier. David writes in the Psalms about how stress affected his emotional being, as well as affecting him physically. However, unlike Epizelus, David had found the best cure and that was to fully trust in the Lord for his "recovery."

During the Iraqi War, I was a Navy chaplain who dealt with Sailors, Marines, Soldiers and SEALs who suffered from PTSD. I found that often the root cause was an overwhelming sense of guilt for something they had seen, done or not done. It was in this light that I remembered how David coped with his trauma by seeking the help of the Lord. In many of the Psalms where David did this, the Hebrew is emphatic and used intensive language and syntax to emphasize David's plight, as well as seeking God's strength and power to overcome any adversity he had. For example, In Psalm. 31:14, David puts his trust in God. The word for trust used is "*batach,*" which means "to totally trust God at the expense of other truth." In every case, his steadfast trust resulted in David being restored in his mind, body and soul because of his love and faith in the God who created him. So, if you have gone through or are going through some traumatic event in your life, do not discount the goodness of God and trust Him to help you overcome all things.

21

CLEON

> "Words from the mouth of a wise man are gracious, while the lips of a fool consume him; the beginning of his talking is folly and the end of it is wicked madness. Yet the fool multiplies words. No man knows what will happen, and who can tell him what will come after him."
>
> ECCLESIASTES 10:12–14

In 425 BC the Athenians had just defeated the Spartans at the naval Battle of Pylos. They had been at war for a while and each side was tired of the conflict. The Spartans made a rare appeal for peace, but the Athenians didn't know how to proceed from there because Sparta had never asked for it. It was uncharted territory for the Athenians. Perplexed, the Athenian council met and included all the citizens of Athens. During the meeting, the Athenian general Nicias spoke in favor of peace, as he was the one in battle the most and had the most to lose. However, his political opponent Cleon on the other hand opted to keep on punishing the Spartans and wanted to destroy their ability to wage war and to have the Spartan menace gone forever.

Cleon had never commanded an army nor ever fought in the war, so he was very open to sending others to fight his battles. He was very good at being an armchair quarterback and used his oratorical abilities to convince men to keep the war effort going. Unfortunately, he was a better speaker than Nicias, so he won the argument, convinced the citizens of Athens to continue the fight and even managed to have Nicias banished. At the urging of

Cleon, Athens continued the war and eventually it was defeated, while Cleon was killed in battle at the head of his men.

Thucydides, who wrote the *History of the Peloponnesian War,* described with rancor what he thought of Cleon. In brief vernacular he said, "He was the first to speak loudly in assemblies and hated the people ... To his political enemies, he would lift his garment and shake his hips as an insult." In short, Cleon was a degenerate, but people still followed him to their own destruction. In the verse of the day, there is a stark contrast between the words of a fool and a wise person.

It is said of those who think they understand war are ready to put others in harm's way, while the soldier or warrior which has the most to lose in war is a little wiser for this reason. Of course, wisdom comes from the Lord and those who follow God and His ways are prudent in their advice. Fools on the other hand, use any means to sway other foolish people, which of course, leads often to their own destruction. Fools, like Cleon will see judgement, and this is also the lesson for us today because God has promised those of us who follow Him will not only have eternal life, but the peace that passes all understanding which comes with wisdom.

22

LESSONS IN LEADERSHIP

> "He who dwells in the shelter of the Most High Will abide in the shadow of the Almighty. I will say to the LORD, 'My refuge and my fortress, My God, in whom I trust!' For it is He who delivers you from the snare of the trapper and from the deadly pestilence."
>
> PSALM 91:1–3

During the Peloponnesian War (431–404 BC), the Athenians established a colony in northern Macedonia for the purpose of utilizing the forests of that area for timber harvest to build their navy. Their presence threatened the already vulnerable Macedonian kingdom of King Perdiccas II, so an uneasy alliance was made with King Perdiccas and Sparta, Athens's main enemy. The only problem was Perdiccas was also in the middle of a war with the Illyrians (modern Albania). So, when the Spartan general Brasidas arrived in the area known as Lyncestis (northern Macedonia) in 423 BC, there was a hostile, foreign army waiting to destroy his small force. The Spartan men were terrified of their new enemy, but Brasidas, using his quick wit and knowledge, encouraged his men with this speech as reported by Thucydides (4.126):

> The present enemy might terrify an inexperienced imagination; they are formidable in outward bulk; their loud yelling is unbearable;

> and the brandishing of their weapons in the air has a threatening appearance. But when it comes to real fighting with an opponent who stands his ground, they are not what they seemed; they have no regular order that they should be ashamed of deserting their positions when hard pressed; flight and attack are equally honorable with them, and afford no test of courage; their independent mode of fighting never leaving anyone who wants to run away without a fair excuse for doing so.

With knowledge of strategy and daring, the Spartan contingent was able to escape relatively unscathed. Brasidas was able to save the day through his leadership and ability to motivate his men by his speech.

Some leaders have that ability to move others and history records many such events. However, in the verse of the day, the Lord reassures those that rely on Him for protection in times of great danger, have the greatest promise for help than any human speech could ever accomplish. This promise can be a comfort for those facing certain danger or even death and was the same passage I used to pray for those going into battle when I was with the Marines during the war in Iraq. No person knows the future, but it is always a positive thing to ask the Lord for help in times of great uncertainty. While there are no guarantees of the outcome, just like the Battle of Lyncestis was for Brasidas, the Lord is a far better strategist and motivator. In fact, Romans 8:31 reminds us that "if God is for us, who can be against us?" Added to that truth is the promise that with Christ, we are more than conquerors. However, unlike the fickleness of humans, God is always true to His Word. With this promise, one should never fear what lies ahead.

23

THE EAR OF DIONYSUS

"For the LORD loves justice and does not forsake His godly ones; They are preserved forever, but the descendants of the wicked will be cut off. The righteous will inherit the land and dwell in it forever. The mouth of the righteous utters wisdom, and his tongue speaks justice. The law of his God is in his heart; His steps do not slip."

PSALM 37:28–31

Thucydides writes in his masterpiece *The History of the Peloponnesian War,* that the Athenians invaded Syracuse in 416 BC. They had been at war with Sparta for years and needed help from their kinfolk in Sicily. When those in Sicily refused to help their "cousins" in Greece, the Athenians sent a huge invasion force and went to war against their fellow countrymen in Syracuse. The war went back and forth for a year until the Athenian navy made a desperate maneuver and put all men and material in their ships and invaded Syracuse from the harbor. After a long, protracted defense, the Athenian navy tried to escape the harbor, only to find out the men of Syracuse had put a long chain around the mouth of the harbor. As the Athenian ship tried to escape, they were trapped by the chain. Seven thousand Sailors and Soldiers were taken prisoner and put into the rock quarry now known as the "Latomie dei Cappuccini" (the quarry of the Capuchins).

In the entrance of the old quarry is a natural formation known as the "Ear of Dionysus." The formation is an entrance to the cave of the rock quarry which is shaped like a tear. The defeated Athenians were placed in the quarry pit to work the stone, but they were not given any food or water. They were to die, a fitting end to their treachery against their relatives. Other accounts tell of how the Syracusan women would go down to the quarry and view the once handsome Athenian men and taunt them by throwing scraps of food and watching them fight over it. Stories abounded concerning the stench from the rotting corpses left in the quarry. The ones who came to conquer and abuse were instead themselves victims of their own pride and arrogance.

The theme of fighting against injustice and the evil that precedes it is a theme as old as the fall of humanity in the Scriptures. There will always be evil on this earth until Jesus comes and sets up a just world in His kingdom. While we crave after justice against evil men, it is often fleeting in this life. However, keep in mind there will always be for those people a day of reckoning. In the verse of the day, God Himself is the everlasting and great judge and will make sure those who follow Him will see His glory in judging evil. In the meantime, it is up to us to fight as much as we can because even though the battle belongs to the Lord, God still uses us to accomplish His will. Like David against Goliath or like the ancient citizens of Syracuse, the battle will not be easy and sometimes may not go like we want it. So, rather than complain about the state of evil in our nation and world, take God at His word. Fight by praying, fight by taking a stand against evil and all that it represents and finally, fight by doing that which is right and don't give into despair or apathy. Remember to keep the law of God in your heart and your steps will never slip. God's justice will prevail!

24

XENOPHON AND THE GREAT ESCAPE

"A leader who is a great oppressor lacks understanding, but he who hates unjust gain will prolong his days."

PROVERBS 28:17

One of the great leaders of the ancient world was a Greek general named Xenophon (b. 430 BC). He was a contemporary and friend of Socrates and was present as a young man in Athens when there was a lot of political scandal, such as the return of the Athenian politician Alcibiades, the overthrow of the thirty tyrants and the Trial of the Six Generals after the Battle of Arginusae (406 BC) at the close of the Peloponnesian War. All of these events left an impression on how he viewed government and how people should let themselves be ruled by others. His writings were required reading for many in higher education for centuries and laid the foundation for many of our Founding Fathers' impressions on what kind of government we should have. However, his life had other aspects to it that had more immediate consequences for those living around him.

He was first and foremost, a military person. There was a civil war between the Persian king Artaxerxes II and his younger brother, Cyrus the Younger. Cyrus hired many Greeks as mercenary soldiers, and under

Xenophon's leadership they were successful. The war came to a head when the forces of Cyrus almost conquered Babylon, but Cyrus was killed in the Battle of Cunaxa in 401 BC. It was here where Xenophon wrote in his classic work *Anabasis,* and he tells of how 10,000 Greek soldiers were able to dodge the rest of Cyrus's army in their trek back to Greece despite being hunted with an army 10 times its size. The work reads like an adventure novel with all sorts of daring do and outwitting the enemy at every turn. It is still studied and commented on by historians and military planners alike.

Xenophon later went on to write about many extraordinary things, but what was striking was his humanity for his troops during this "Great Escape." People respected him and understood that he cared for his people, having proved it despite the danger. It was genuine (or so it seemed) and that is why his name is associated with lessons in positive classical history.

In the verse of the day, Solomon reminds us of the importance of having good leaders. That starts with us praying to the Lord and asking Him to protect us—individually and corporately as a nation, as well as sending us leaders who have personal spiritual character, in addition to leadership capabilities. We need to ask God to send us leaders like Xenophon, who are smart as well as caring for their people. But we should also pray for God to send us men and women who are guided by the Lord's Holy Spirit and who seek after His wisdom.

25

WHAT HAPPENED TO LYCURGUS?

> "'Let us rejoice and be glad and give the glory to Him, for the marriage of the Lamb has come and His bride has made herself ready.' It was given to her to clothe herself in fine linen, bright and clean; for the fine linen is the righteous acts of the saints. Then he said to me, 'Write,' *Blessed are those who are invited to the marriage supper of the Lamb.* And he said to me, 'These are true words of God.'"
>
> REVELATION 19:7–9

Among the writings of Plutarch (d. AD 119), he tells the story known as *The Life of Lycurgus* about the origin of Spartan society and law. Lycurgus is the one who is given credit for the reforms that turned Sparta into a military society in ancient Greece. Part of the story of how he did this was he went to the Oracle of Delphi and the god Apollo appeared to him and told him he needed to go back to Sparta and change its laws and institute a new government. With those marching orders, as the story goes, he gathered 30 of his comrades and went into the marketplace and took over the city by force. This was the story that was told over the centuries in Sparta, but the only problem was that there was never any man in history which fit this story. Even

Plutarch, writing centuries later after the demise of Sparta, begins his story in the first paragraph with the disclaimer that there is no proof of Lycurgus.

However, one aspect of the story of Lycurgus was the start of the Spartan custom of what is known as the "Syssitia." This is where all men of Sparta would join in a great banquet hall at mealtime and share a meal together. Of course, this shared experience and communal meal built friendships and camaraderie that added to the warrior ethos of Sparta. All men were expected to contribute money, goods in the form of food and services to keep the mess hall going and those who didn't were kicked out of being a citizen of Sparta. Men formed "mess-hall clubs" which were the front runner of guilds and even ended up having athletic contests based on different clubs. The formation of this was the center and heart of Spartan society.

With this background knowledge, it is easier to understand the references to the "Marriage supper of the Lamb" in the verses of the day. In the case of a Christian, this is the consummate event for a believer. It is an occasion in the future where Jesus Christ Himself, will call all Christians together and have a wedding celebration such as has never been prepared!

We, as Christians have a special relationship with Christ through the Church and in Ephesians 5:21–32 we look forward to a time in the future when this marriage will take place. This is the wedding feast found in Revelation 19:7–9 and it is a time of great joy when all of our expectations of being with Christ in holy matrimony will be concluded. The Syssitia of Sparta will be nothing compared to the glory and majesty found at the Marriage of the Lamb! No need for any wedding crashers, admission is free with a "repentance of sin" ticket, freely given by the Lord Jesus Himself.

26

SOCRATES AND THE POWER OF WORDS

> "For the word of God is living and active and sharper than any two-edged sword and piercing as far as the division of soul and spirit, of both joints and marrow, and able to judge the thoughts and intentions of the heart. And there is no creature hidden from His sight, but all things are open and laid bare to the eyes of Him to whom we must give an account."
>
> HEBREWS 4:12–13

Many of us know the phrase that kids often say in response to someone who has said something hurtful: "Stick and stones may break my bones, but words will never hurt me!" Such are the words and philosophy of youth, because words really are powerful and, indeed, have been the cause of many wars. Hurtful words have also been the reason for many who have retreated permanently from a once close relationship with others. At worse in some instances, a false tale can even put someone to death. Take for instance, the reason why the ancient Greek philosopher Socrates (d. 399 BC) was put to death for his teachings on the ancient gods of their day.

Socrates and his philosophy have been one of the major influences in Western thought. As a young man, he was a war hero and had the respect of both young and old of the men of Athens. He never wrote his ideas down, but they have been passed down to us by many of his students and acquaintances, especially Plato. Socrates is best known for what is called "the Socratic method" by which he would ask a question and then his students would respond. In their response, he would then use guided practice to lead them to the right conclusion. His insight into life was ridiculed by all "civilized" society of the Athenian democracy and there were even plays written to mock his ideas. However, it was his words against the common belief that the anthropomorphic (the belief that non-human things have human characteristics and traits) gods had human vices that brought him further scorn. He believed they did not and taught the young men that. For his different views on the gods, he was accused of the crime of asebeia, or the teaching of false ideas about the gods. For this he was tried, convicted and forced to drink poison hemlock.

The idea of bantering around exaggerated words from uninformed people is nothing new. We have seen examples of people running for public office making wild claims of unreal comparisons of their opponents with historic madmen in our elections history. Words mean things, but with wild claims and rhetoric, people fall prey to tempestuous moods of the mob. Used wrongly, this is a dangerous thing and can make even the most passive individual hateful and can potentially cause violence to others.

The reason why words are so powerful is found in the verse of the day. It is because it goes into the inner person and stirs the emotions which in turn cause excitement. For this reason, God desires for us to read His Word because it *is* powerful and reaches into the deepest part of who we are as people and allows us to see reality as it truly exists. The standard of reality is how God made it and the only way to know the fullness of reality is, is to know Christ.

27

PLATO'S MORALS

"I am the good shepherd; the good shepherd lays down His life for the sheep. He who is a hired hand, and not a shepherd, who is not the owner of the sheep, sees the wolf coming, and leaves the sheep and flees, and the wolf snatches them and scatters them. He flees because he is a hired hand and is not concerned about the sheep. I am the good shepherd, and I know My own and My own know Me, even as the Father knows Me and I know the Father; and I lay down My life for the sheep."

JOHN 10:11–16

In reading Plato's *Republic,* there is one lesson that sheds light on who we are before God and as Americans. One of the first things that Plato tackles in his work is the idea of who sets the standards of morality and right and wrong in society. Whether it's a city or country, he believes that whoever is in power are the ones to determine what is just and unjust. From there, those in power rule only at their own advantage over those who are *not* in power, kind of a "survival of the fittest and strongest" mentality. For those people, they will do anything to keep their power.

Furthermore, any laws they yield must be made with the intent of keeping power, even to the detriment of those not in power. Taxes, customs, societal mores, customs and cultures, and even individual freedoms are unimportant luxuries except for those in power who control all aspects of these over the masses. Under the pretense of "caring" for the people, the few in power control goods, food and freedoms for all and by doing this, hold the "mob" captive. Like the line in the movie *Gladiator,* the senator talks about the plan of the evil emperor Commodus, when he says: "He will bring them death them [the masses], and they will love him for it!" This is the reason why governments have come and gone because this is the mindset of those in power in history. Except for a few nations, including the United States.

To understand this truth, one must understand our history, which is a national belief in the God of the Bible. In the verse of the day, Jesus talks about His sheep and how He will protect them. While other governments have a few who hold power, America is different in that power rests with the people.

However, while those in power rule over people and determine what they believe is just and true like what Plato proposes, Christianity holds people together because it gives a standard which is far superior to anything humanity can develop. Jesus's sense of justice and love goes to the heart of who we are as humans and it is that standard which both ruler and ruled are held accountable, not the fiat of those in power. This truth also transcends even those who God calls to rule over us in government, for they are held accountable by the same God; thus all sides are satisfied with working together, under God.

28

PLATO AND TRUTH

> "In the LORD I take refuge; How can you say to my soul, 'Flee as a bird to your mountain; For, behold, the wicked bend the bow, they make ready their arrow upon the string to shoot in darkness at the upright in heart. If the foundations are destroyed, What can the righteous do?'"
>
> PSALM 11:1–3

In Plato's *Republic,* Book Two, Plato makes a case about how truth needs to be protected from the onslaught of those who would promote lies. Truth in a society is important according to Plato because without it, "a man cannot flourish and realize his fullest potential from his natural gifts." Those who can be truthful in this type of a setting make for a special type of man. As Plato writes about this type of man: *He is* "a perfect guardian of the state and will be able to be philosophically high spirited, swift and strong." Lofty ideals indeed! Furthermore, he makes the comparison of a trained dog which is generally friendly to his master and the dog, and his master has a special bond of friendship. However, that same trained dog is just the opposite to a stranger. For this reason, Plato suggests that like the dog's reaction to a stranger, that is how we should treat someone who brings up a desire to change the meaning of truth and wants to introduce some strange idea against that truth and beauty.

Thankfully, our Founding Fathers understood the classics and the different forms of government from the past. From kings, dictators, tyrants, oligarchies, democracies and republics, they hammered out what is the best form for America. This was discussed and written about in detail in the Federalist Papers, especially in #18 and #19 where examples of ancient Greek governments were discussed and shown how a people need to have something which would give individual freedom but still hold together under some type of crisis. Fortunately, they chose a republican form of government which gives power to the people, as long as the people remain interested, informed and free from immorality.

This is where the brilliance of the Founding Father's plan came into play. They knew that an informed electorate armed with the knowledge of God would understand right from wrong and truth from error. As the inner voice of God speaks in our hearts because we are made in the image of God, even though that image is marred, we still have a sense of justice from injustice and right from wrong. The verse of the day is a reminder that there are those who will pervert truth and bring darkness, but God rewards those who seek after His righteousness. From God's truth, we build on a foundation. Without God's truth, there is no truth; there is only the opinion of a person. For this reason, each of us must continue to pray for truth as we are led by God's Spirit in all things pertaining to our lives and our nation.

29

PLATO AND THE IMPORTANCE OF THE PERFORMING ARTS

"Lamech took to himself two wives: the name of the one was Adah, and the name of the other, Zillah. Adah gave birth to Jabal; he was the father of those who dwell in tents and have livestock. His brother's name was Jubal; he was the father of all those who play the lyre and pipe."

GENESIS 4:19–21

In Plato's *Republic,"*he deals with specific traits and responsibilities of the citizens that are necessary for good government. The early part of the work is not so much a treatise on what is the best and most efficient form of government's (i.e. democracy, republic, dictatorship, etc.) way to rule people, but what important characteristics are needed by its citizens for that society to flourish and prosper. One of those characteristics is his writing on the importance of the performing arts: drama, comedy, sculpture, music, and athletics.

For example, with respect to drama the author extols the virtue of learning about the human condition through the medium of theater. In plays we are warned of the dangers of an evil person who has no character versus someone who uses their abilities for good. Through music, we learn that there is the ability to reach deep into the soul and that therefore it should be used for promoting virtue in individuals to serve their culture's greater good versus those who use it for selfish desires. Music is a powerful means to either corrupt society or to enhance it and should not be abused. As a result, it should be regulated by good social mores to keep it pure. Lastly, the use of athletics is needed to not only enhance the body, but to teach the young person to combine soul and body for the purpose of discipline for the greater good of society in general. I remember that as a youth in a public school these Greek ideals were taught by some of my teachers who understood what a liberal arts education means. However, with the cultural drift through the decades of modernism and postmodernism, educators replaced godly virtues in our public sectors with a different educational model that does not promote virtue or biblical values. As a result, for example, music that appeals to our base desires is promoted and exalted instead of being used as a tool to teach discipline of body, soul and spirit.

This is exactly what happened in the verses of the day. When Cain and his offspring went away from God, music discovered by Jubal was used for evil. That line of people in Genesis 4 and then in the line of Genesis 5 all were evil according to the declaration of God in Gen 6:5–6 because "every thought of his heart was evil continually." In Genesis 1–11, we have a biblical narrative of God's extreme wrath against humanity due to its excessive sin. Music is just one example of something that can be wrongfully used. Human nature has a way of taking something good and corrupting it. Each of us has a preference, but the point for today is that we should ask ourselves this question: Does the music we listen to help our soul for good and bring us closer to praise and worship God? If it does, great! If not, well that is between you and the Lord, just don't let your music become a stumbling block.

30

PLATO AND PROTECTING OUR YOUTH

> "Let the glory of the LORD endure forever; Let the LORD be glad in His works; He looks at the earth, and it trembles; He touches the mountains, and they smoke. I will sing to the LORD as long as I live; I will sing praise to my God while I have my being. Let my meditation be pleasing to Him; As for me, I shall be glad in the LORD."
>
> PSALM 104:31–34

In Plato's *Republic,* the philosopher tackles the topic of "bad narratives." That is when a person puts out a story, work, or writing that is blatantly false and after some investigation, is found to have a morally corrupting influence on the youth. Plato then builds a case where these types of negative inducements aimed at youth have a terrible effect on society because youth do not have the full capacity to understand the nuances of allegory and reality. Plato even goes so far to say that these narratives are ugly and because they lack beauty (a word meaning a positive message) for youth, should not be allowed.

Even the ancient pagans understood the importance of teaching positive messages to children. It wasn't so much Plato extolling censorship, but rather discussing the positive results of this kind of teaching for society. Plato suggests, even teaching the classics of Homer at a young age is not the best idea because it deals with complex themes, like hatred, revenge, and manipulation. He argues instead that fables which teach children right from wrong and good from evil are the best means to be used in the younger ages.

Contrast this proven idea which held sway in Western society for centuries, with the current thought in our public educational system today. Instead of protecting our children, we have exposed them to numerous evils in the name of learning. Worse yet, we have taken the crown jewel of the definition of beauty, the mention of God, out of the narrative. Plato goes on to say that if one does tell an evil narrative, they are to sacrifice a pig and expect a youthful listener to later "commit the foulest of crimes."

I once had a very wise pastor who said "protect and teach your children in the ways and teachings of the Lord and His glory. People may say you are sheltering your children, but believe me, as they get older, they will learn the ways of the world. At least when they get older, they will at a minimum know the difference and at that time, they are accountable to God for their actions." While that may seem simplistic, there is a truth to the statement. In the verses of the day, teaching the proper view of God for an adult as well as a child demonstrates a positive, edifying message that builds up all of humanity. From the child to the adult, being taught to appreciate God's beauty in all things, whether found in His Creation, or taught through art and music will nurture a positive outcome in people. The wonder, nature, and character of God is something virtuous and should be taught.

31

PLATO AND THE ELITES

"Thus you will know that I am the LORD; for you have not walked in My statutes nor have you executed My ordinances but have acted according to the ordinances of the nations around you."

EZEKIEL 11:11–12

In Plato's *Republic,* the great philosopher spends a great deal of time setting up what he believes are the qualities essential for citizens to make the ideal government work. After a long discourse on morality, Plato shows great insight into how the Greeks viewed the soul and its relationship to how people make wise and proper decisions based on virtuous education. This was accomplished physically through gymnastics and through morality as depicted through the arts. After he has established in his mind the ideal man or woman, his treatise then takes a wild and unexpected turn. It is the stuff that reminds me of the thinking of contemporary far left progressives in government.

Once the perfect citizen is put forth, then he goes into how that citizen is supposed to owe his or her allegiance to the city (or the "State.") In doing so, there is no private property or ownership of goods. Everything is held in common for all. Even children are wards of the state and are supposed to be brought up by everyone. There is no family structure and men and women have sex only during approved yearly approved "Festivals." If men and women have sex at other times, and if there is a child, the unapproved baby must be terminated. The family structure is frowned upon because people in a family are more loyal to each other than the state. For the state to be supreme and people loyal to it, the family must go. Of course, the people who run the state are the ones who are the elite who know what is best. At least that is what Plato presents in the rest of his thesis. At the top of the social strata are "the philosophers."

Plato's statements are a reminder to us that no writing other than the Bible fully contains truth. As seen in earlier pages, Plato has some good ideas, but his writing also has some bad ideas and ideas that conflict with the Bible. We must read and study with wisdom and through the lenses of Scripture and a biblical framework.

Nations that promote biblical values thrive; nation that do not do so fail. As the verse of the day shows us in God's decrees: "I am the Lord your God!" This statement is found in Ezekiel 67 times alone. God is supreme, not the state– or even the family. The Lord made the family (Gen. 2:23–25) and it, not the state, is the "backbone" of all civilization. Furthermore, the Lord reminds us in Ezekiel that it is He, not us who sets the agenda or in this case- "ordinances" regarding what is right and wrong. Only those societies that have exalted the position of the Lord in its hierarchy and worshipped God freely are the ones who have prospered and have freedom. May we be so wise.

32

LEONIDAS AND PELOPIDAS

"But Jael, Heber's wife, took a tent peg and seized a hammer in her hand, and went secretly to him and drove the peg into his temple, and it went through into the ground; for he was sound asleep and exhausted. So, he died. And behold, as Barak pursued Sisera, Jael came out to meet him and said to him, 'Come, and I will show you the man whom you are seeking.' And he entered with her and behold Sisera was lying dead with the tent peg in his temple."

JUDGES 4:21–22

Right after the Peloponnesian War (circa 400 BC), Thebes and Sparta were allies. However, now that the war was over, Sparta was jealous of Thebes and while the Thebans were having a celebratory feast, King Leonidas of Sparta took a small retinue of men and captured the city of Thebes. In the conflict, a few men from Thebes escaped and fled to Athens. There the Theban leader Pelopidas made plans to make his city of Thebes free once again from the dastardly Spartans.

The plan of Pelopidas was to interact with Leonidas with the pretense of peace, but while he was in negotiations with the Spartans, Pelopidas was secretly planning to send a small contingent of soldiers and sneak them into

Thebes. The plan was to have a friend of Pelopidas who still lived inside of the city hold a drunken feast and invite the Spartans under the pretense of friendship and get them drunk. Then, when all were drunk, he would let Pelopidas and his men into the city. When all the Spartans, except for Leonidas (who did not drink alcohol) were drunk, Pelopidas's friend opened the gates and let in his fellow Thebans. They soon retook the city, killed all the Spartans, and regained their freedom.

In the verse of the day and in the historical story, both told stories of trust and or stories of subterfuge. All of us have experienced an event of betrayal from someone we trusted, only to be shocked to see how wrong we had misjudged the person. Not only did we misjudged someone; we felt hurt because of the betrayal. Spiritually, that will never happen to those who have put their trust in God because it is not in His nature or attributes to betray us. Sure, there will be times that we don't understand how He is working, but we can always rest in the fact that in the long term God's love for us will fully manifest itself at the end when we have the complete story and understanding of the big picture. If you are going through a difficult time, keep your faith intact and rest assured that someday you will not only understand, but love God even more for working out all things. Remember, living life is a marathon and not a sprint!

33

ELEKTRA AND THE GREEK TRAGEDY

"Then his brothers also came and fell down before him and said, 'Behold, we are your servants.' But Joseph said to them, 'Do not be afraid, for am I in God's place? As for you, you meant evil against me, but God meant it for good in order to bring about this present result, to preserve many people alive. So therefore, do not be afraid; I will provide for you and your little ones.' So, he comforted them and spoke kindly to them."

GENESIS 50:18–21

In the tradition of the ancient tragic Greek plays, one story that has continuous consequences is the story of Elektra. Two Greek playwrights who wrote about this story were Sophocles and Euripides and while they both wrote about the same character, there were differences in each of their portrayals of the story.

The story begins with their father King Agamemnon sacrificing Elektra's sister Iphigenia at Aulis to the goddess Artemis because he had killed one of Artemis' sacred stags. Agamemnon was the head of the Greek army on the way to fight the Trojans and because of his dastardly deed, the gods gave contrary winds to the Greeks. To the utter contempt of his wife,

Clytemnestra, and against his wishes, he was forced to sacrificing Iphigenia, to get favorable winds.

Agamemnon went on to fight for 10 years in the Trojan War. In the meantime, Clytemnestra, to prevent any potential sacrifice of herself and Agamemnon's remaining children, sent Iphigenia's sister, Elektra, and her brother Orestes away from Agamemnon to a secret place. When the Trojan War ended, Agamemnon came home and when he least expected it, was killed by his wife while he was taking a bath. Only then did she feel her revenge against her husband was complete. However, when Elektra found out what her mother had done, she spent the last days of her life plotting and executing her revenge on her mother for killing her father.

The lesson for those of us who know and love God is found in the proverb, "there is enough blame to go around for everybody." From a biblical perspective, one sin can have dire consequences throughout a family or even a society. One can easily follow how Agamemnon's original sin of sacrilege against Artemis continued through the entire family and ended up destroying lives. This is the way of the world! There must be a better way and that can be found in the idea of forgiveness as seen through the eyes of God. In the verses of the day, Joseph recalls the day how his brothers sold him into slavery and how even though it was a long road, he was eventually vindicated and was able to be a vessel of the living God for good. When he had the opportunity to get his revenge after his father died, his brothers feared he would take revenge. Instead, Joseph showed life through the eyes of God, forgave, and understood how even the most tragic events of life can have a godly conclusion.

34

PELOPIDAS AND CAUTION

"So his servants took him out of the chariot and carried him in the second chariot which he had and brought him to Jerusalem where he died and was buried in the tombs of his fathers. All Judah and Jerusalem mourned for Josiah. Then Jeremiah chanted a lament for Josiah. And all the male and female singers speak about Josiah in their lamentations to this day. And they made them an ordinance in Israel; behold, they are also written in the Lamentations."

2 CHRONICLES 35:24–25

Plutarch writes about a leader of the ancient Greek city of Thebes by the name of Pelopidas (d. 364 BC) who was one of the few leaders who cared for those he led. Born into a wealthy family, he gave away his wealth and resources to feed the hungry, while he lived a subsistence lifestyle. He never had any scandals and rose above any problems by being a problem solver, rather than causing them. A natural leader, all loved him because he was someone they trusted and were willing to follow him without hesitation.

As a young man, he and Epaminondas (a future general and statesman of Thebes) fought side by side and both almost died, but the experience made close friends of them for life and together they accomplished much.

At the Battle of Leuctra (371 BC), the Theban army led by these two finally broke the hold of Sparta over all the Greek city states. It was Pelopidas as an ambassador to Persian at the court of Artaxerxes II (Ezra 7:1) who made peace with Persia. It was Pelopidas who taught Alexander the Great's father Philip the tactics of war. Unfortunately, his preference to lead is what eventually killed him for in battle he saw the enemy general and went after him without help from his army. Pelipodas was greatly outnumbered and died from his numerous wounds.

Plutarch writes about how foolish this once great leader was and how he deprived the rest of his people of his wisdom and leadership due to his lack of discerning the moment. One can say the same thing about good King Josiah in the Bible. In the verses of the day, Josiah got involved in a battle against the Egyptians because they had to go through his country. It was a hasty decision because the real enemy was Babylon and Josiah paid the ultimate price. After his death there were a series of bad kings which led to Israel's demise. The point of today's thoughts is to look before you leap. Don't get into a conflict unless you are positive the Lord is on your side, and you are not doing it because of your own passion. Make sure to count the cost of your efforts. Most of all, be wise as a serpent, but harmless as a dove (Matt 16:10). Trouble will naturally find you out if you are faithful to the things of the Lord, but if something comes up, seek the will of God in your prayers before you do something rash which will affect others.

35

AGESILAUS II AND TITHES

> "But you say, 'How have we defiled You?' In that you say, 'The table of the LORD is to be despised.' 'But when you present the blind for sacrifice, is it not evil? And when you present the lame and sick, is it not evil? Why not offer it to your governor? Would he be pleased with you? Or would he receive you kindly?" says the LORD of hosts.' 'But now will you not entreat God's favor, that He may be gracious to us? With such an offering on your part, will He receive any of you kindly?' says the LORD of hosts."
>
> MALACHI 1:7–9

Right after the Peloponnesian War (431–404 BC), Sparta was the undisputed leader of the Greek-speaking world. It was during this time that the Spartan king, a man by the name of Agesilaus II (d. 360 BC) ruled. He had a deformity in one of his legs which by all accounts of Spartan law he should have been killed at birth, but for some unknown reason, the elders decided to let him live. As he grew, he still participated in all the Spartan rituals of soldiering and even excelled in them, earning the respect of friend and foe alike. What started as a most unlikely life ended up becoming Sparta's most famous king. However, he was also responsible for Sparta's eventual demise due to his hatred of Thebes.

During his reign, Sparta took a position of military conquest throughout Greece. One of the bloodiest battles during his reign was the Battle of Coronea (394 BC), which was against the city-state of Thebes. Thebes opposed the growing power of Sparta and at this battle both sides lost heavily, but the victory went to Sparta and in gratitude Agesilaus gave a tenth of the spoils of the conflict to the Oracle of Delphi. However, twenty years later, Thebes took revenge and defeated the Spartans at the Battle of Leuctra (371 BC) and ended Spartan domination in the Greek world for good. Perhaps Agesilaus should have remembered to try and bribe the oracle of Delphi for another victory?

For the ancient Greeks, tithing was a bribe or a way to curry the favor of the gods for future blessings. In short, a payoff for some position of power over others. In the Bible, the idea of tithes is something altogether different. Tithing is something for the people of God to remember that any blessings they have in their lives is because of the direct goodness of God working in their lives. However, in the verse of the day, the people of God only went through the motions of worshipping God and gave the Lord the worst, instead of the best of their flocks for sacrifice. Fortunately, God doesn't work like that in the New Testament because He was the one who was the perfect sacrifice, but the concept is still there. As a result, we should always have a heart of worship by praising God for His goodness to us, as well as remembering our gratitude.

36

DION

"Who is like the wise man and who knows the interpretation of a matter? A man's wisdom illuminates him and causes his stern face to beam."

ECCLESIASTES 8:1

In ancient Syracuse, Dion was a man who lived by platonic philosophy, meaning there was realism in the midst of idealism. Dion was a friend of the tyrant Dionysius I, the leader of the free city of Syracuse. However, once Dionysius died, Dion tried to gain control of the town and unfortunately for him, Dionysius II became the Tyrant of the city. This was unfortunate because Dionysius II was considered an imbecile, and a drunk and only cared for pleasure. Realizing he would never become the leader, Dion nevertheless felt it was his duty for the sake of the citizens to help train and teach the young Dionysius to be a leader.

Regrettably, there were bad friends of the new tyrant who saw Dion as a threat, and they did what they could to discredit him. Although he had a thorny personality, he still was the best hope for the city, but many plots were laid against him to discredit him. One such plot was led by a man named Sosis who ran naked in the city streets covered in blood. He screamed that Dion was after him and he needed help. A city meeting was called and upon greater inspection, it was discovered all Sosis's wounds were self-inflicted. Even so, Dion was a controversial figure and the townspeople figured where there was smoke, there was fire. As a result, Dion was banished from the city by Dionysius II.

Upon first glance, many believed the lies that Sosis told about Dion. It was only upon greater inspection and discernment that the false plot was discovered. In the Scriptures, Proverbs talks about the simple and how easily they are fooled. However, the Bible is very clear that those who have a close walk with the Lord have wisdom and the ability to discern right from wrong. It is this wisdom that people receive from God Himself when a person trusts Christ as their Savior because the Bible says we can possess the mind of Christ (Phil 2:4–7) through the indwelling of the Holy Spirit. Besides this privilege, God gives wisdom freely to those who ask for it (James 1:5–6). For this reason, those who are Christians are called upon to use this wisdom to interpret the world around them. As one does that, we can see beyond deception and do what is right before the Lord. Try this and you will find yourself better off than if you never ask God for help.

37

IPHICRATES AND LEADERSHIP

" ... nor do you take into account that it is expedient for you that one man dies for the people, and that the whole nation does not perish."

JOHN 11:50

In Plutarch's work *The Age of Alexander,* he tells a story of an ancient Athenian general named of Iphicrates (418–353 BC). He was a commander in the era of the ancient Greeks who was especially known for his knowledge of training and handling of light infantry. He compared the light armed troops as the hands, the cavalry to the feet, the main body of infantry to the chest and breastplate, and the general to the head. It was this last statement that is especially interesting.

Because the head is so important to the function of the entire body, it should be protected because the rest of the body depends on it. However, the problem with Iphicrates was he was not a man who was cautious in battle. He took numerous chances. His doom was foreshadowed when the Oracle at Delphi prophesied of his death in battle. When he heard this, he brushed it off and simply replied "The fate of Sparta does not lie in the life of one man!" Although brave, he soon died in battle doing what he always did–taking unnecessary chances. Unfortunately, when his men saw he was dead, they lost heart and soon lost not only the battle, but their lives.

In the Bible verse above, we read of the plot to kill Jesus from the lips of the enemy, Caiaphas. He naively thought that by killing Jesus, he would wipe out his adversary. However, this is a stark example of sinful humanity trying to get rid of God. Like the prophecy at Delphi about Iphicrates, one man does make a difference. While taking out one man seems like a simple solution, the truth is God is eternal and resolute, and no plot of people will succeed against His decrees. God used the foolishness of humans, to accomplish His perfect will of sending Christ to the cross. Even though Christ willingly went to the cross and was raised from the dead, the Holy Spirit soon followed for all of humanity for those who put their trust in Him. It is this God given power that God has given to us to continue the work of the gospel to a lost world that needs the saving power of Jesus Christ. Unlike Iphicrates who died from foolishness and couldn't lead, let yourself be guided by the Holy Spirit and unleash the power to lead in this world for the glory of God today.

38

TIMOLEON THE JUST

"Tell us by what authority You are doing these things, or who is the one who gave You this authority? Jesus answered and said to them, I will also ask you a question, and you tell Me: Was the baptism of John from heaven or from men?" They reasoned among themselves, saying, "If we say, 'From heaven,' He will say, 'Why did you not believe him?' But if we say, 'From men,' all the people will stone us to death, for they are convinced that John was a prophet."

LUKE 20:2–7

In the world of the ancient Greeks, Timoleon (d. 337 BC) stands first among equals. Born into one of the leading families of Corinth (the same city that the apostle Paul ministered four hundred years later), Timoleon was known as a lover of freedom and fairness. He put this ideology over friendship and family and although he supported his elder brother's coming into power, he opposed him when his brother became corrupt. Things came to a head with his brother and eventually, Timoleon was involved in a plot to have his brother killed. Tragic as that was, it built trust between him and the men of Corinth. So much so that when Carthage took over all the Greek cities of Syracuse, they elected Timoleon to lead the men against them in war.

The historian Plutarch tells us that as a clever man, Timoleon led an effective campaign against the enemy by his ability to unite the normally factious Greeks into a formidable fighting force against Carthage. For instance, once when he was doing a recon mission to see the strength of enemy forces, he ran across a donkey caravan carrying loads of parsley. His men took this as a bad omen because parsley was usually used to decorate dead men's tombs. However, Timoleon reminded the men that in times past it was also used in the Isthmian Games as the garland used for crowns of victors. He then took some of the parsley, made a crown and wore the laurel on his head. All his men then took some parsley and did the same. Once everyone had a garland on their heads, an eagle carrying a snake appeared out of nowhere and dropped the dead snake into the men's group. This was considered a good omen. Timoleon and his men were then victorious after that.

In the verse of the day, Jesus took on the entire religious system of the Sadducees–namely the high priest, elders and scribes and took an argument they had and turned it against them. While they wanted to trap Jesus and make Him look like a fool in front of the people, He was able to use the argument and show their lack of understanding of God's will and goodness for them. God sent them John the Baptist as Elijah as part of the fulfillment of the Messiah (Mal 3:1), but they refused to believe it because it didn't jive with their preconceived idea of what their idea of spiritual reality. That is why we need a Timoleon or godly people to be used of the Lord to be truth tellers to the masses. Only those who see things from God's perspective will be given total victory over this evil world and time!

39

TIMOLEON TO THE RESCUE!

"For the sorrow that is according to the will of God produces a repentance without regret, leading to salvation, but the sorrow of the world produces death. For behold what earnestness this very thing, this godly sorrow, has produced in you: what vindication of yourselves, what indignation, what fear, what longing, what zeal, what avenging of wrong! In everything you demonstrated yourselves to be innocent in the matter."

2 CORINTHIANS 7:10–12

Timoleon (d. 337 BC) was a man born during the right time and place. The city of Syracuse in Sicily was founded by the men of Corinth during the 8th century BC. Since then, there was a kinship between the two cities, but while Corinth flourished due to its international trade and good leadership, Syracuse was run by a series of oppressive tyrants. These tyrants had caused the people of Syracuse to not only be oppressed politically but also caused abject poverty because of the corruption. In an act of desperation, the men of Syracuse appealed to the city of Corinth for help against getting rid of their tyrants, once and for all. Unfortunately, in their weakened state, the nation of Carthage was waiting to take over Syracuse.

The men of Corinth meanwhile had voted to help their cousins, the Syracusans, but the leader, Hicetus of Corinth, had been in secret negotiations to have Carthage work together to overthrow the tyrants in Syracuse. Timoleon was called upon to help because he was deemed an honest man. However, he had for the past twenty years withdrawn from all public life and leadership due to his heartbreaking fight with his big brother. Years earlier, he supported his big brother to be the new leader of Corinth, but his brother turned out to be wicked and after numerous innocent people were murdered, Timoleon plotted in his beloved brother's assassination for the good of the city. It broke his heart, and he withdraw from all public service for twenty years. However, at the insistence of the people, he left his personal grief, came out of his own comfort zone and because of his sense of duty, once again became the general for the army to liberate those at Syracuse.

For the rest of his life, Timoleon was involved in the war. His exploits in and around the events of the war were exemplary and he made a difference in the life of those who lived in Sicily. Space here prevents going into all aspects of his leadership, but of this reading is that despite his own personal anguish, he was led to help others.

In the verses above, Paul had sent a letter to the church at Corinth. The letter had done its job because it caused the people to stop and think and repent of what they were doing. This was a good and godly repentance because it seems that it caused a true, inner, heartfelt repentance to understand their sin before a holy God. It was repentance not that they had been caught doing something wrong, but a realization that they had offended the Lord Himself. From there, an inner introspection followed with an action of changing their behavior. It is that realization of regret for their past actions which caused a change in their lives that we focus on here. May you pray and realize your actions before the Lord today!

40

ALEXANDER'S LEGACY

"Many plans are in a man's heart, But the counsel of the LORD will stand."

PROVERBS 19:21

There are many lessons for us from the life of Alexander the Great, perhaps the greatest Greek of all time. By the time Alexander the Great was 32 years old he had conquered one third of the civilized world. A brilliant strategist and tactician, his leadership inspired his men to march over 17,000 miles in 8 years. While his military exploits were legendary, his empire soon died after his death. His greatest contribution, however, was his legacy found in a process known as "Hellenization." This is a term which describes how Alexander left Greek culture and cities in his wake. For instance, he created 70 cities and left behind advanced studies of botany, medicine, astronomy, and Greek philosophy. To the first legacy historians and military analysts marvel, to the second we still feel the practice and daily effects of Greek culture.

Each of us touch each other in some way. We leave our imprint on others by how we talk and live. In the verse of the day, only what the Lord says really matters. Like Alexander's temporal military exploits, we live our lives in the short term, and it affects those around us. However, the question being raised today is: what is the verdict on your life in the long run?

Will people remember you in a good, positive way or something else? Better yet, what does God think of how you have conducted yourself according to His counsel?

The Lord's ways sometimes run into conflict with the wisdom of this world, but ultimately you must decide if you want to leave a good permanent legacy or temporal destruction. What will your legacy leave and what will be remembered? Only one life will soon be past, only what's done for Christ, will last. May God's grace be with you today.

41

ALEXANDER AS A YOUNG MAN

"The mind of man plans his way, But the LORD directs his steps."

PROVERBS 16:9

Alexander the Great was one of the best generals and military leaders of all time. As a youth he was trained by Aristotle and learned the warrior code from his father, Philipp II of Macedon. During his time with the great philosopher, he was taught botany, astronomy, architecture, and many other subjects. It was here that he was first given the idea of spreading Greek culture (called "Hellenization") and science throughout the world. Another thing engrained in his mind at this time was the Persian menace. Persia had invaded Greece time and time again for the past two hundred years, so Alexander wanted to rid his world of this problem once and for all. As a result, even though he was only 18, he had a 4-part plan to defeat and consolidate this vast enemy empire.

When most of us were 18, we wondered what our life would become. Alexander didn't have that problem. At that age he worked his master plan by defeating his close enemies in Greece and united all Greeks with a common cause. Then he set about to destroy the Persian Navy because they were lifeline of the Persian army. His third phase was to actively engage and defeat the Persian Army and lastly, it was to consolidate the whole Persian Empire under a Hellenistic umbrella. Through hard work, brilliant tactics, and diligence, he was successful and by age 32, he had not only conquered the known world but had Hellenized it.

Even though this task seemed impossible at the time, Alexander accomplished his dream and vision. It took him the rest of his short life, but he achieved his boyhood goals. On a much smaller scale, each of us should have a plan to live our lives and part of that plan should be to serve God in one way or another. All of us of course have dreams, but some individuals are more proactive in pursuing them. Some on the other hand, just wait for life to "happen." In the verse of the day, we can plan, but we must all remember that the Lord has some say in what really happens.

Some of the most frustrating moments in life come when we have plans and they don't work out. If that happens, step back and listen to the still, small voice of God. Perhaps He is trying to tell you something. Be patient and eventually the truth will come out. Pray. Meditate. Ask God for direction. Then proceed. As you go, learn to hear what God is telling you and unlike Alexander, you will live long and prosper! Oh, and along the way make sure to thank God for the peace only He can give you.

42

ALEXANDER AND THE PERSIANS

"For you yourselves know perfectly that the day of the Lord so comes as a thief in the night. For when they say, 'Peace and safety!' then sudden destruction comes upon them, as labor pains upon a pregnant woman. And they shall not escape."

1 THESSALONIANS 5:2–3

For centuries the Persians and Greeks had experienced war with each other. When Alexander the Great decided to end the tension once and for all, he faced a formidable enemy. Persia ruled almost the entire civilized world and had great resources and a huge military complex. Darius III was the king, and his generals first met Alexander's army at the Granicus River in northwest Turkey in 334 BC.

Assuming Alexander would be tired from marching all day, the Persians rested for the battle which was sure to take place the next morning. It was here where we first see the genius of Alexander. The Persian generals were resting on a superior fighting position on the hills above the river. Furthermore, their 4 to 1 advantage gave them a false sense of security. They had their cavalry near the river in case of any fast attack while their infantry was on top of the hills. When Alexander came upon this situation and saw how unready his opponent was for battle, despite marching all day and having tired troops, he quickly formed his army together and rushed the Persians.

Darius's generals, in a false sense of security, had neutralized their cavalry because there wasn't anywhere to maneuver. Also, the infantry was of no use because it took such a long time to form up and meet the enemy down the hill. These factors made the odds even as the Greek phalanx's long spears held the Persian horses at bay. The battle was fast and furious as Alexander thrust his spear into the face of the king's son-in-law Mithradates. Alexander himself was knocked off his horse and an axe split his helmet in two. Over the course of the battle though, Alexander broke through the defenses and caused the Persian army king to flee. Quick action and thinking on his feet had caused the defeat of a much larger army.

I hope and pray that in many respects we are not like Darius III's generals. Oftentimes we have a sense of security that is false. While they thought their army was invincible, they overlooked the obvious. Let us not forget our strength does not lie in our technology, military or way of life. Our security lies in our relationship to God. As we have a biblical perspective and live according to what is pleasing to Him, we possess a perspective that makes us wise. Human wisdom only has knowledge for what can be seen. God's wisdom not only includes the perception of man's knowledge, but the ability to see the whole situation. Let us not say "peace and safety," from a human perspective, but rather let us seek after the whole counsel of God and know true safety and wisdom comes from a holy and perfect God who cares for us.

43

ALEXANDER AND DETERMINATION

"And when I came to you, brethren, I did not come with superiority of speech or of wisdom, proclaiming to you the testimony of God. For I determined to know nothing among you except Jesus Christ, and Him crucified."

1 CORINTHIANS 2:1–2

After the Battle of Granicus (334 BC), Alexander the Great (d. 323 BC) took a detour in the pursuit of his opponent Darius III of Persia by marching south into Judea. As he marched his army, a tempest caused him to stop at the port of Myriandrus (near the biblical city of Antioch) and take refuge. He left his wounded men there and when the deluge let up in the morning, his tired and wet men continued their march south. Unknown to Alexander at the time was the fact that Darius was only 15 miles away on his rear. When the Persian army marched into the port city, they captured and cut off the hands of all the wounded men of Alexander's army. When he found out, Alexander and his able-bodied men were infuriated. Thinking this was a trick, he didn't believe the reports, so he wanted to find out for himself.

He requisitioned a picket boat in the middle of the night and spied the atrocities on his men from his vantage point on the dark sea. Helpless to assist them, he went back and used this as a tool to whip his men into a frenzy of revenge against the enemy. Despite his army's fatigue, they marched back a few miles toward the port into a narrow strip of field between large hills about a mile and a half wide and waited to do battle with the Persians. The location was called Issus, and it became the beginning of the end for Darius. Some estimates of the battle say that Persia lost about 100,000 men to Alexander's loss of only 300. This, of course, is an exaggeration, but the battle was a massacre and caused Darius to flee for his life.

Despite having a tired and worn-out army due to "circumstances of God," Alexander was able to use it to rally and make his troops more determined than ever to wreak havoc on the Persians. Determination is the key word in this context because by taking a bad situation, Alexander was able to turn it into something that made his men strong.

It is this same word of determination that Paul used in the verses of the day encouraging the Corinthians (and us) to be faithful witnesses to the Lord. What the word means is "to separate" and is usually the word used in the Bible for judgment. However, in this context it means that like Alexander's men, they were so focused on defeating the enemy that nothing else mattered. In the same way, we as Christians need to be so focused on the things of God, that nothing else should interfere with our dedication and faith in Him. If one were to go into the context of Paul's declaration of determination here, nothing should get in the way of our love for God. Only then will we see how our faithfulness and love for the Savior will give us a victorious life in all things.

44

ALEXANDER AND TACTICS AT ISSUS

"For You have maintained my just cause; You have sat on the throne judging righteously. You have rebuked the nations; you have destroyed the wicked; You have blotted out their name forever and ever."

PSALM 9:4–5

In 333 BC, the forces of Alexander the Great met the might of the Persian Empire under King Darius III. Up to this point, Alexander had defeated his generals at the Battle of Granicus, but Darius was eager for a rematch. For his part, Darius had been planning and training his army for such a time as this. Estimates put his army between 200,000 and up to 600,000 troops. Darius, however, was overconfident because of his military might over the Greeks because they only had 40,000 total. Darius knew that Alexander would fight.

Darius had a large army, so Alexander set the battlefield in a narrow place to discourage any mobility the Persians might have. By putting the battle in a narrow bottleneck, Alexander nullified any advantage Persia had over him. It was here his disciplined tight knit, but slow-moving phalanxes wiped out the compact Persian lines because they couldn't move out of the way. As Alexander changed tactics, the Persians couldn't adapt, and the Persian lines collapsed. When this happened, Alexander went straight for the Persian king.

Sensing a danger of being trapped, Darius fled with many of his senior officers. After the battle, the Greeks were sifting the goods in the Persian camp. It was here that Alexander and his men found Darius had left his wife, mother and two daughters behind. This was advantageous because when Alexander treated Darius' wife with kindness, she was more than willing to help him and instrumental in explaining Persian thought to him. This became a huge strategic boost to the war for him against a much larger enemy force.

How often have we planned and schemed for things to happen in our favor. In the world, the term "politics" is often a euphemism for doing what one needs to do to get an advantage over others. It is a game that sinful people play. However, sometimes there are situations where we have no control over things and God has His perfect will for some other outcome that we never considered. That is why we should remember that it is God who sets up and destroys things and regardless of we do, it is He who has His perfect will. If you find yourself in this type of a situation, just accept the fact that God has His way and don't fret or get frustrated. While we like to manipulate and control, it is God who accomplishes His perfect will. The lesson is for us to be wise and accept some things without getting upset and angry. Darius tried to win the day and he ended up losing everything. Trust God and be content with the outcome!

45

ALEXANDER AND THE LUNAR ECLIPSE

> " ... giving no cause for offense in anything, so that the ministry will not be discredited, 4 but in everything commending ourselves as servants of God, in much endurance, in afflictions, in hardships, in distresses, in beatings, in imprisonments, in tumults, in labors, in sleeplessness, in hunger, in purity, in knowledge, in patience, in kindness, in the Holy Spirit, in genuine love, in the word of truth, in the power of God;"
>
> 2 CORINTHIANS 6:3–7

One of the most important battles in history was between the armies of Alexander the Great and Darius II of Persia. After a series of earlier battles between the two, Alexander had the upper hand, but at what is the northern part of Iraq at a place called Arbela, the fate of the western and eastern world was determined here in October, 331 BC. Darius had everything to lose and his gamble of putting his entire force against Alexander here was a momentous decision. Things were going his way as he moved his army into place until 11 days before the battle when a lunar eclipse occurred.

At the time, the eclipse was understood by the Persians as imminent danger because that is how their leaders interpreted the event. Meanwhile, for the Greek army of Alexander, it was interpreted to be a spiritual sign of victory. For their part, fear spread throughout the Persian army. Most of the men became dejected and afraid. Conversely, the Greeks were encouraged and confident of success. When the two armies finally met, Alexander's army won the day, not only inspired by heavenly signs, but also by the battlefield genius of Alexander. It was after this battle that Alexander rode into the capital of Persia three weeks later as the victor, while Darius was killed by his generals and his broken army stayed in hiding.

In contemporary society, signs and omens are laughed at as being simple superstitions. However, in some cultures today, these are still seen as having some spiritual significance over people's lives. We do know that there were some heavenly events which preceded the birth of Jesus. It's interesting how some can take the same heavenly sign and come up completely different interpretations of it. As a result, how should we as Christians see those things that affect both our physical lives and the spiritual world? In the biblical verses above, the best way to approach things is to understand there may be something to spiritual signs and wonders, even if they are demonic or heavenly. Also, realize not everything is all physical and understand there is a spiritual side to life. However, most of all, the result of knowing reality is the recognition that the Lord God, in the Persons of the Father, Son and Holy Spirit is the first and ultimate authority of both the physical and spiritual realms! As a result, we need not fear that which we do not understand for if God is for us, who can be against us?

46

ALEXANDER SLEEPS IN

"But You, O LORD, are a shield about me, my glory, and the One who lifts my head. I was crying to the LORD with my voice, And He answered me from His holy mountain. Selah. I lay down and slept; I awoke, for the LORD sustains me. I will not be afraid of ten thousands of people Who have set themselves against me round about."

PSALM 3:3–6

In the early morning sun in 331 BC at Gaugamela (modern northern Iraq), the troops of Alexander the Great had risen hours before. They had prepared their horses and sharpened their swords for the dangerous battle before them. They were going to face the Persian hordes of Darius III. It was the second and final battle between the two kings outside of the modern Iraqi city of Mosul which became known as the Battle of Gaugamela. Estimates of the Persian army's strength ran as high as a million troops, among other implements of war, such as war elephants and chariots. However, the apprehension of the common soldier of the Macedonians was extremely high, because their commander, Alexander the Great had yet to awaken and take charge. It was midday, and no one had yet seen him. Perhaps he was ill. Rumors were rampant.

To tell the truth, he overslept. He slept like a baby until he finally awoke and came outside. He was surprised that his men had never woken him because of the importance of the day. However, when asked how he could sleep with the stress of the upcoming battle his response was simple. "I have complete confidence in my paternal general of the calvary, Parmenion."

Oh, that we would have the same confidence in our God! King David shows this same confidence in God when he was running from his son Absalom. As he writes in Psalm. 3: "I lay down and slept." Despite deadly enemies which hunted him, David knew God would protect him. In fact, in the context of Psalm 3, David likens his impending doom like a toothless wolf outside the camp trying to scare people. Now that is faith in action. Here in America, the main cause of death is heart attacks, and the main cause of heart attacks is stress. It is for this reason in the verses of the day; we need to see and re-assess our lives in relationship to God. God not only is our Savior, but also the blessed controller of all things. He is God and all things are controlled by Him. In fact, Romans 8 tells us that "if God be for us, who can be against us?" Remember that truth when you are being tormented by stress and worry. Remember, a toothless wolf will howl, snarl at you and look ferocious, but cannot do anything to you. Be at peace!

47

ALEXANDER AT GAUGAMELA

"O that You would slay the wicked, O God; Depart from me, therefore, men of bloodshed. For they speak against You wickedly, And Your enemies take Your name in vain. Do I not hate those who hate You, O LORD? And do I not loathe those who rise up against You? I hate them with the utmost hatred; They have become my enemies."

PSALM 139:19–22

As noted earlier, In 331 BC, the forces of Alexander the Great met the entire might of the Persian Empire under king Darius III for a second time. Prior to this armed meeting, Alexander had never lost a battle and the previous time he met Darius in battle, he not only defeated him at the Battle of Issus in 333 BC, but also captured Darius's wife and two daughters. Darius had been planning and training his army for a large battle. Estimates put his army between 200,000 and up to a million men. Included in this number were numerous war elephants and 200 scythed chariots. Darius picked the battlefield and even had his men clear field of shrubs and trees so he could use these chariots and allow his men room to maneuver.

At Issus, Darius had a large army but could only partially engage Alexander's army because there wasn't any room to maneuver. Now, at the

Battle of Gaugamela (331 BC), Alexander added another challenge to the tactics of Darius III; Alexander changed tactics and went straight for Darius and the leadership fled, leaving behind his wife and family. This time Darius learned from his previous mistake and wasn't going to get boxed in. His plan was to extend his lines, so he could use all his army and cavalry. However, Alexander anticipating his enemy's strategy, used his Phalanx to his advantage by making them use 23-foot-long spears called sarissas. A phalanx was a group of ten men across and sixteen men deep in close quarters, armed with a shield on the left arm and the sarissa on the right. They marched in formation and were able to take on cavalry, infantry, and chariots head on.

Alexander's phalanxes were able to punch a hole through Darius's thin line, making an opportunity for Alexander's fast cavalry to pursue Darius and his royal retinue. He also kept behind some reserves to keep Darius's army from flanking him. This worked perfectly and once again, Alexander was victorious. Finally Darius fled and the Greeks won the day. After Darius fled, he was killed a few days later by his angry cousin. Like many who brag about how great they are, everything he had lived for and built was for nothing. However, the same thing happened to Alexander when he died young at age 32. All this shows that regardless of what great thing humanity may do or build, it is like sifting sand. In contrast, Eternal God is Lord over all time, and He always has the final say. Consequently, consider what is important in this life and because God has the final say on things, a good recommendation for us all is to put all our energy where we join the army of God and His Son, Jesus Christ. He wrote the book on superior strategy and will always win.

48

ONE LAST THING ABOUT ALEXANDER

> "But Michael the archangel, when he disputed with the devil and argued about the body of Moses, did not dare pronounce against him a railing judgment, but said, 'The Lord rebuke you!' But these men revile the things which they do not understand; and the things which they know by instinct, like unreasoning animals, by these things they are destroyed."
>
> JUDE 9–10

On June 13, 323 BC, Alexander the Great died in ancient Babylon at the young age of 32 and at the height of his dominion. When he died, there was a mad scramble from his generals over who would claim the body. Whoever held his body could make a claim to be Alexander's heir to the empire and thus hold the keys of great power. After much deliberation and manipulation, a minor general, by the name of Perdiccas, seized the body, took control, and became the supreme commander. After making a grand gold-covered mausoleum with wheels Perdiccas headed back to Macedon to bury Alexander and proclaim his new empire.

However, it was not to be. Another general named Ptolemy, kept an army in what is now Turkey and when the cart bearing Alexander's body came through the town, raided the funeral party, stole the body and headed for Egypt, where Ptolemy ruled. Perdiccas then gathered an army, but after many attempts failed to get his prize back. After many setbacks and in frustration, Perdiccas' men mutinied and eventually killed their leader. So much for visions of power for the unfortunate Perdiccas.

This may give some insight into the event of Jude 9–10 between Satan and the archangel Michael. Moses died on Mt. Nebo and was buried and apparently Satan had the same idea that if he controlled the body of Moses, many would follow him, instead of God. While it may seem difficult to see how this could happen, it was the intent behind the scheme that God wanted to nip in the bud. The evil of men's hearts is to plot and connive and that is why God sent Michael to expose this evil and stop it from ever happening. As believers, we must always be on the lookout and actively stop any plot that goes against the goodness of God! The lesson of Jude is not only to expose evil, but to stop it cold in its tracks. Vigilance is the key and through God's leading, revealed by prayer and His Holy Spirit, we must seek to always do good. Then, and only then, will people like Perdiccas in our world today be silenced forever.

49

DEMOSTHENES AND THE POWER OF THE SPOKEN WORD

" ... for I do not wish to seem as if I would terrify you by my letters. For they say, "His letters are weighty and strong, but his personal presence is unimpressive and his speech contemptible."

2 CORINTHIANS 10:9–10

When I was a young boy, I had a speech impediment of a lisp. My friend Jeffrey could not pronounce his "R's" and so we became best friends in speech class. With the speech therapist's help, I eventually lost my lisp, and Jeffrey could pronounce his "R's." While good for us, the best speech success story of all time goes to an ancient Greek by the name of Demosthenes. He was a sickly boy, so athletics was out of the question. However, he instead turned to studying and working on not only how to speak properly, but also in the construction of speech. (He had a bad habit of breaking up his sentences to breathe which was very distracting.) It is said that he put pebbles into his mouth so he could enunciate his words properly.

He literally spent years perfecting his delivery, but he also worked on the construction of public speeches. His speaking was considered so perfect, that he is given the title "the father of all orators" by other great speakers such as Cicero, Caesar, and many others. He had numerous techniques which would draw his listeners in, such as telling a short story, changing the pitch and tone of his voice, or even appealing to certain aspects of a person's emotions. All these techniques focused on the delivery of the speech; but he was also careful about the construction of his arguments to maximize the effectiveness and intent of his topic. Unfortunately for him, his greatest target was Philip II of Macedon, the father of Alexander the Great. Eventually, Philip died (assassinated in 336 BC), but his son, Alexander, sent one of his men to arrest the famous speaker, but rather than be arrested, Demosthenes committed suicide.

The spoken and written word has enormous power when used properly. Words can be powerful. In the classical era and for many centuries following, rhetoric was an essential part of education. This was the case in ancient Rome during the first century with the education of the Apostle Paul. Except in his case, he himself writes in the verses above about his "contemptible speech." This doesn't mean that Paul had a speech impediment, but rather, when he spoke people would roll their eyes and not listen because of the way it was presented as well as the content of the speech. In the original language construction of this phrase, people would be instantaneously turned off by what Paul had to say. In other passages, Paul often made a point that it wasn't the skill of how things were said, but the content it contained (I Cor 1–2). In other words, it is God's Word(s) that has meaning and power, not the person who speaks them. For this reason, anyone who remembers and quotes God's Word has authority and power which shows that the power is with God, not in the skill of the person bringing the message. As a result, let God use you!

50

DEMETRIUS CHANNELS THEMISTOCLES

> "Inasmuch as these people have rejected the gently flowing waters of Shiloah And rejoice in Rezin and the son of Remaliah; 'Now therefore, behold, the Lord is about to bring on them the strong and abundant waters of the Euphrates, even the king of Assyria and all his glory; and it will rise up over all its channels and go over all its banks.'"
>
> ISAIAH 8:6–7

After Alexander the Great died in 323 BC, his four generals divided up his empire. However, to do that, the generals would have to fight it out with the city-states because, sensing freedom, they formed an alliance and fought against Alexander's former general Ptolemy. For the Greeks' part, they sent the son of the Athenian leader, Demetrius, a young, but brilliant hero of the Athenian aristocracy to confront Ptolemy. According to Plutarch, as found in *The Age of Alexander,* Demetrius was trounced by Ptolemy in Syria, but was the hero of the day at the naval Battle of Salamis (306 BC), outside of modern Athens.

This was the same site where, centuries earlier, Themistocles had defeated the Persian king, Xerxes (480 BC). There was an island with a narrow channel and the channel was easily defended on both ends. By using the same tactics as Themistocles, Demetrius easily defeated the combined naval forces of Ptolemy. However, once defeated, Demetrius buried Ptolemies' war dead with full military honors. Not only that, but for the 1200 prisoners he had captured, he gave them food and clothing and set them free. This is not the typical way to treat one's enemies, and it raises the question: why was there a war fought in the first place? The answer is found from Ptolemy's statement to Demetrius during this struggle, "This war was fought more on honor and power than for life and death." Having defeated Ptolemies armies, the Greeks enjoyed freedom, even though it was but for a short time.

In the verses above, the people of the nation of Judah had been given peace by God. The phrase "the gently flowing waters of Shiloah" depicts the peace and quiet of the pool of Siloam in Jerusalem in stark contrast to the raging waters of the Euphrates River. It is a metaphor that the peace given by God to Judah was rejected and replaced with war with other nations. For sinful reasons, nations like power over peace and that is the reason nations go to war. God is a God of peace for those who follow Him and those who are led by ungodly leadership find only death and destruction. God does judge those nations that are for shedding blood; but favors those nations who are willing to fight for what is right. As long as there are sinful people in this world, war is a reality. However, it is only through embracing the things of Christ that this cycle be broken. May we pray for a peaceful solution to this problem. Only by prayer will a gracious God give a good solution.

51

THE LAMIAN WAR

> "But when Jesus heard this, He said, 'This sickness is not to end in death, but for the glory of God, so that the Son of God may be glorified by it.' Now Jesus loved Martha and her sister and Lazarus. So when He heard that he was sick, He then stayed two days longer in the place where He was."
>
> JOHN 11:4–6

After the death of Alexander the Great in 323 BC, Athens was ready to make war against Macedon, the home of Alexander the Great. Alexander had forced Athens and other Greek city-states to be a part of a military coalition which when they worked together, successfully humbled the Persian Empire. However, the forced obedience of Athens by Macedon left a sour taste in all freedom-loving Greeks and at the first opportunity, they made war against Macedon. This was known as the Lamian War or Hellenic War (323–322 BC).

An aged Athenian leader named Phocion opposed the war, but a young general named Leosthenes convinced the rest of the city-states to enter the war. Phocion warned the people that they had no money, resources, weapons or men for a sustained effort and they would lose the war against the hardened Macedonian combat veterans. As he is recorded saying: "They (the young men) were in a sprint, but I'm afraid this effort will be a long race," reasoned the elder statesmen. Time proved him correct. Athens enjoyed some initial victories, but eventually Leosthenes was killed, and Athens and its Greek allies were defeated. Athens after that was never again a force to be reckoned with, either financially or militarily. The war had changed Greece forever.

In the verses above, the story focuses on one of the greatest miracles that Jesus performed during His earthly ministry. In the context of the story, Jesus was almost attacked and stoned a few days earlier when he visited Jerusalem and preached a sermon. To avoid confrontation and be safe, He and His disciples fled for a couple days, during which time His friend Lazurus died. Despite knowing the danger and his impending death, He wanted to show His disciples and others His power over life and death. We know that because in verse 4, the original language of "so that Son of God may be glorified," has what is called a "*hina* clause," which means "with the express purpose of ... " In other words, Jesus raised Lazurus from the dead with the express primary purpose of showing God's glory to those who saw it.

Like Phocion who allowed Leosthenes to go to war to prove a point, Jesus waited a few days to prove His power over death to others by doing it in a powerful way. One takeaway from this encounter is that God often allows something to happen in our lives, which while we may pray for Him to take it away from us, will in the long run demonstrate His power by working through our situation.

52

PHOCION AND THE GOOD WIFE

"He who finds a wife finds a good thing and obtains favor from the LORD."

PROVERBS 18:22

Many of us have heard the saying "behind every good man is a woman." This was certainly true in one instance in ancient Greece where a leader of the city-state of Athens known as Phocion (c. 402 BC–318 BC) had a wife who was known for her wisdom. Even though Phocion was a good man, full of integrity in the eyes of the Athenians, his standing as a statesman was increased immensely by the efforts of his wife, the humble daughter of a commoner. They worked well together. He was in the public eye and she was constantly at his side, telling others that she was simply "the ornament' of Phocion. Of course, it wasn't true, but in their culture, her words were wise. Even though never mentioned by name by Plutarch, he tells a simple story of her virtue.

A director of a play wanted a chorus of real women (men usually played female actor's parts then) dressed in costly ornate dresses to sing in the background of his play. However, the producer told him the idea was frivolous and too expensive. This caused a heated discussion, and the director was rebuked and silenced. In protest the director, who was also the moderator of the play, refused to go out on the day of the performance and stood on the side of the play, out of view of the audience. When the producer came out to tell the director to go out, they had a loud shouting match which was heard by everyone. Finally in exasperation, the producer told the director, "Don't you see Phocion's wife out there, everyone knows she always goes out with only one maidservant to wait on her? Why should you give yourself airs and turn all our wives' heads with your extravagance?" The conversation was heard by the audience, which immediately exploded with loud applause.

Of course, most events in our lives are not as dramatic as those of Phocion and his wife, but this and the verse of the day remind us of the importance of having a good wife. In the verse of the day, the word for "find" is a word which means the person seeking a wife must actively seek after finding not only a wife, but a *good* wife. It is the same word and context used in Deuteronomy 4:29 where a person after suffering for a while, actively seeks God and God in His mercy and grace tells the person he will find Him. This type of finding is for the one seeking a wife, not to be taken in by beauty, sex or other means. It is based on the character and nature of that wife that God grants his favor to the man who has actively sought for such traits in a future mate. Given this sage advice from Proverbs, those who are married should take time today to appreciate their spouse and if there are children in the family, they should be taught the importance of seeking a spouse, a wife in this case who is virtuous and loves God.

53

A PYRRHIC VICTORY

> "For by You I can run upon a troop; And by my God I can leap over a wall. As for God, His way is blameless; The word of the LORD is tried; He is a shield to all who take refuge in Him. For who is God, but the LORD? And who is a rock, except our God, ... "
>
> PSALM 18:29–31

Pyrrhus of Epirus (319–272 BC) was one of the ancient world's most famous and talented generals. He was raised with a sword in his hand as he fought and learned about warfare during what was known as the Wars of Succession (also, Wars of the Diadochi, 322–281 BC), after the death of Alexander the Great in what is now Greece and Macedonia. As a young man, he was known for his prowess and bravery under battle conditions. These wars helped him develop strategies which would help him later in his military campaigns against the Romans.

Pyrrhus was one of the few Greeks who realized that the Romans presented a future danger because of their desire for expansion. As a result, he was determined to prevent future Roman aggression. He set out with his army and campaigned in Rome and successfully defeated larger Roman armies at the Battle of Heraclea (280 BC) and the Battle of Asculum (279 BC). However, after the second battle he famously said: "If we are victors in one more battle with the Romans, we will be utterly ruined." This is where the phrase a "Pyrrhic victory" came from and it means that even though someone won a battle, victory came at a great cost and any further action would be devastating.

Eventually, Pyrrhus, fearing having to engage in war with both Rome and Carthage, withdrew back to Epirus. He was killed in a city skirmish there where he was fighting an enemy soldier and an elderly lady dropped a stone on his head from above, killing him.

Pyrrhus spent almost his entire life fighting. He also made some bad choices for friends, allies, and wives (he had three) and through a lot of betrayals and intrigues, his life was constantly in turmoil. As a young man he had the strength to defeat his enemies, but when he got older, it was more difficult. Finally, after a lifetime of war and political infighting, he died never really knowing peace.

Throughout our lives, we will have ongoing struggles and we may often lack the strength, resources, or knowledge to successfully deal with them. Although Pyrrhus learned how to deal with adversity, he never learned how to ask for help and as a result, the constant battles wore him down. As Christians, we can be like Pyrrhus and fight our own battles, or we can turn to the Lord and have Him teach us how to deal with problems. Whether through work, family or other circumstances, if a person is right with the Lord, God is the One who gives us the strength and know how so we can be victorious. Sure, we may win in our own strength, but after fighting in our own strength we will eventually grow weary. So, we can have a Pyrrhic victory, or simply ask the Lord for help. May you choose wisely.

54

VIRGIL'S "AENEID OF AENEAS"

"By this, love is perfected with us, so that we may have confidence in the day of judgment; because as He is, so also are we in this world. There is no fear in love; but perfect love casts out fear, because fear involves punishment, and the one who fears is not perfected in love."

1 JOHN 4:17–18

In the Latin epic Roman poem written by Virgil, "The Aenid," written between 29 BC and 19 BC, the poet looks back to Greek history and mythology and describes how the Roman people came to exist as a race of people. From the ashes of the destruction of Troy at the hands of the Greeks, Aeneas escapes death at the end of the Trojan War and is commissioned by the god Jupiter (Jove, and Zeus in Greek mythology) to take a handful of people and start a new civilization on the other side of the sea. This begins a series of events which eventually brings Aeneas to Rome. One of the events of which Virgil writes describes one of the great love stories of the ages – the meeting of Aeneas and the queen of Carthage, Dido.

Led by Venus and Juno, Aeneas washes ashore near the city of Carthage where Dido finds him and nurses him back to health and gives him shelter and food. He tells her of his adventures, and she is struck by the handsome stranger and welcomes him into her city and life. Eventually, they become intimate emotionally and physically. As time goes on, he is content and develops a real love for Dido and forgets his duty to Jupiter until one day he is reminded what he needs to do and returns to his original purpose and duty. Without saying goodbye to Dido and explaining himself, he leaves her and goes on to finish his quest. She is devastated over her loss and seeming betrayal and kills herself. Before she does so, in her grief, she curses Aeneas and all his ancestors, thus setting up the age-old wars that will follow between Carthage and Rome.

In this tragic story, we have human free will and the interaction of the gods of ancient mythology. In Greek and Roman religions, like most religions, humans are merely pawns in the game of life at the whim of the gods. However, in Christianity it is entirely different. Although God is all powerful and all knowing, He proved His love for us by willingly dying for us to forgive our sins. In this love, however, He was the one who provided the means of forgiveness by providing Himself as the substitute for of our salvation and the object of our love. Unlike the fickle Aeneas who forsook Dido, God would never do that. As we put our faith and love in God, He is faithful and will never leave us or forsake us ... and that is a promise from the true God who created the heavens and the Earth.

55

AENEAS AND KING LATINUS

> " ... and when they arrived, they went into the synagogue of the Jews. Now these were more noble-minded than those in Thessalonica, for they received the word with great eagerness, examining the Scriptures daily to see whether these things were so. Therefore many of them believed, along with a number of prominent Greek women and men."
>
> ACTS 17:10–13

Many of us are familiar with the story of the Trojan War, during which the Greeks defeated the Trojans after which the Greek hero, Odysseus had a long quest back to his home in Ithica. However, many don't know about what happened to the Trojan side of the story. To make a long story short, there was a survivor of the destruction of Troy and he and his small band of men barely made it out of the conflict alive and he, like his Greek counterpart Odysseus, experienced many things as he sought out a new land to call home.

The story is chronicled in Virgil's *Aeneid*. It is a classic work and when the hero of the story lands in Laurentum, (modern Italy, on the coast southwest of the city of Rome), there is temporary relief and rest for Aeneas and his men. But there are soon new concerns. The locals see the men and arm themselves for a battle. The king is summoned and when King Latinus of

Laurentum, in a verbal exchange with Aeneas, finds out about the trials and tribulations of the stranger, he is visibly moved and offers a refuge for the suffering men. Noticing their noble demeanor, he realizes their value and merit. There are other versions of the origins of the Roman Empire, but I like this one the best because it deals with people at a level that builds, instead of destroys.

The same type of thing happened with the Apostle Paul in the verses above. Having been discouraged from others about preaching the Gospel of Christ, Paul presents a Scriptural case, and the people of Berea respond in faith. Whether because of busyness, work, or life in general, we all have our own journey to travel. However, we also all need to land somewhere where life is stable and welcoming. That place is found in the Lord Jesus Christ. Notice the Bereans accepted Paul's preaching with great eagerness and examined the Scriptures for themselves. We should do the same and be excited about the things of God—therein will we find true rest.

56

PAUL AT MARS HILL

"And they took him and brought him to the Areopagus, saying, 'May we know what this new teaching is which you are proclaiming? For you are bringing some strange things to our ears; so we want to know what these things mean.' (Now all the Athenians and the strangers visiting there used to spend their time in nothing other than telling or hearing something new.)"

ACTS 17:1921

When the Apostle Paul went to Athens, he was taken aback by the prevalence of idolatry. Athens at the time was just a memory of its past glory and all they had were ancient monuments and statues. Not wanting to waste a good opportunity to tell people about Jesus, he went out daily and talked to the people in the synagogues and marketplace; however, not unexpectedly, it caused trouble. In the verse above, the word for "took" means a violent seizure and the word is used numerous times in the book of Acts (16:19, 18:17, 21:30) to note when people were angry and grabbed someone to drag them before the civic leaders for the purposes of punishment on the place of judgement. In this case it was a place known as the "Areios Pagos."

Mars Hill (the Areopagus) in Athens was a place where 100 selected aristocrats and civic leaders determined the fate of the person who was set before them. The place was and still is an unworked marble hill (unlike the beautiful acropolis) where people argued and warred with words (hence the use of the god of war–Ares or Mars) and if determined to be guilty, the council had the power to put someone to death. Paul wasn't there to simply debate philosophy and talk about God or gods as most think, he was put on trial for his life and had to convince them about the validity of Jesus and Scripture. If not, he would have suffered the same fate as a famous philosopher who was tried in Athense for the same reason (introducing a foreign god and corrupting the peace of Athenian society) and by the same council 450 years earlier – Socrates.

Once before the council, Paul was respectful, but his answer showed his command of Scripture and its principles. Without directly quoting passages, he showed how his worldview was steeped in the knowledge and character of God. He mentions how God made the heavens and earth (Gen 1), that He does not dwell in temples (1 Kings 8:27), He gives life and health to all people (Isaiah 42:5) among other examples which show the glory of God. The illustration for us is that when we talk with others, we start with some things we have in common, but then freely in discussion, bring in the wonderful character and attributes of God. God guarantees that His Word will not return void (Isaiah 55:11) and we will be blessed that we have been used by God to glorify Him.

57

ANCIENT CORINTH AND THE BEMA SEAT

> "But you, why do you judge your brother? Or you again, why do you regard your brother with contempt? For we will all stand before the judgment seat of God. For it is written, 'AS I LIVE, SAYS THE LORD, EVERY KNEE SHALL BOW TO ME, AND EVERY TONGUE SHALL GIVE PRAISE TO GOD.'"
>
> ROMANS 14:10–11

If one visits the ancient city of Corinth today, he or she finds the ruins of a once large city where trade and shipping from both sides of the Mediterranean Sea once met. Corinth also had a reputation for being a place where every human vice could be openly found. When trouble arose, those suspected of causing the problem were taken to a place in the city where the leading magistrate would mete out judgement at a place called the "Bema Seat." This was an elevated platform in the city center where public trials were held. An example can be found in Scripture (Acts 18) where Paul was called to answer before the proconsul Lucius Gallio. One can still stand on the very spot today where Paul appeared before the magistrate long ago.

However, the event of Acts 18 is not the focus of this reading. Instead, there is a far greater judgment which will take place in the future, and it concerns us. The Bema Seat during Greek and Roman times was a place not only to give out punishment for crimes, but it was a public place where a leader would make open declarations and even reward those who had done something noteworthy in the community. It was the place where athletes would get rewards or crowns for winning a contest. It was used for judgement and is often translated that way in the Bible, it was also a place for winners to be declared winners. This was often demonstrated by receiving a crown from the king or other leaders.

It is fitting then, that in the future, we as followers of Christ, will go up to the platform of God's throne and be declared winners before all of creation and receive our reward of crowns (2 Cor 5:10). Those who are believers are winners at the Bema Seat. In sharp contrast, those who are not believers will face eternal judgement before the eternal Judge of the Universe. It is a judgement we need not fear because the judgment for sin was already taken care of at the cross and we have already been declared righteous because of our faith in Jesus and His sacrifice as payment for our sins (Rom 5:1–2). It is at the Bema Seat that those of us who have put our faith in Christ will be openly rewarded by the King and Creator of the universe. And remember, it is faith in the atoning death of Jesus Christ on the cross for our sins that unlocks this privilege.

58

THE POLITARCHS OF THESSALONICA

"But the Jews, becoming jealous and taking along some wicked men from the marketplace, formed a mob and set the city in an uproar; and attacking the house of Jason, they were seeking to bring them out to the people. When they did not find them, they began dragging Jason and some brethren before the city authorities (politarchs), shouting, 'These men who have upset the world have come here also ... '"

ACTS 17:5–7

In an area of Greek monuments in the British Museum, stands a marble plaque called the "Politarchs' Inscription." It is an unassuming sign which is perfectly preserved that was found in the 1800s during an excavation of the old city gates of the Greek city of Thessaloniki. It's about two feet long and about 16 inches wide and reads: "The politarchs are Sosipatros, son of Kleopatra and Lukios Pontius Secundus; Aulos Auios Sabeinos; Demetrios, son of Phaustos; Demetrios son of Neikopolis; Zoilos, son of Parmenion and of Meniskos;"

This artifact was the first of 19 other ancient documents found in modern times that speak of a group of city leaders called "Politarchs" (literally, "rulers of the citizens"), who were leaders of major cities in ancient Greece.

For years historians discounted the fact that there was ever such a political office because before the discovery of these artifacts, all evidence had been lost. This skepticism bled over into questioning the reliability of the biblical text because in Acts 17:6 and 8 this word was used by Luke to describe the city leaders in Thessalonica. In short, the inscription proved the biblical record was reliable in this reference.

This brings up the question of whether Christians need to have proof that historical things written of in the Bible are true. While skeptics love to go through and point out passages they believe to be wrong, what about us Christians? Do we blindly believe those things that we can or cannot prove historically or scientifically are true? Well, yes and no. Because the Bible is God's Word, the things contained within it are true, so even though it is not a science or history book, the things it says like the city authorities in Thessalonica are true and therefore we should see any history written in the Bible as true. Likewise, the things about the death, burial and resurrection of Jesus we can believe is a fact and therefore is also true. While we accept this as a fact, we also accept it on faith. While some things cannot be proven empirically by our senses, God made us in His image. It is our spirit that bears witness with God's Spirit that assures us of truth. It's like love, we know it exists, but we cannot touch, taste or eat it. In other words, we believe the Bible because it says it is true, and we take that as fact by faith. Some things can be proven, some cannot; but we rest assured that all of it is God's Word and is true.

59

EARLY CHURCH AND HERODOTUS

"Where is the wise person? Where is the scribe? Where is the debater of this age? Has not God made foolish the wisdom of the world? For since in the wisdom of God the world through its wisdom did not come to know God, God was well-pleased through the foolishness of the message preached to save those who believe."

1 CORINTHIANS 1:20–21

For centuries the name of the Babylonia king Belshazzar was lost to history. He was the party-hearty king of Daniel 6 where God warned him of impending doom with his message on the wall, "Mene, Mene, Tekel, Upharsin." Belshazzar was the grandson of Nebuchadnezzar and son of Nabonidus. There are plenty of records and monuments and literature in antiquity of both kings, but nothing of Belshazzar. The only mention of him in anything was found in the Bible and for two millennia his existence was questioned. Instead of accepting his existence as a fact, many scholars made up explanations regarding the biblical reference to him, or simply claimed that the Book of Daniel as history was fabricated.

Human nature being what it was, claiming the mistake route was the best and easiest because the message of Daniel is prophetic judgment on sin and of course humanity doesn't want to hear that story. So rather than thanking God for giving His Word to us, the Book of Daniel was largely ignored by many biblical scholars and throughout Christendom in general. Even today, many commentaries on Daniel deny it was written in the 6th century BC by Daniel and dismiss it as a "historical fiction." As the saying goes, "ignore it at your own peril." Sadly, this is how many Christians approach the Word of God.

For years, the only evidence we had of Middle Eastern history during this time was the Bible and the writings of the Greek historian Herodotus. For some modern scholars, the writings of Herodotus are considered complete fiction. However, the story of Belshazzar and rediscovering evidence of his name reads like a detective story. It seems the secular sources of history over the years were trying to erase Belshazzar on purpose. Imagine that secular historians purposely leaving things out for a hidden agenda. It seems that when the Persians took over the Babylonian kingdom (read the real account in Daniel 6), they made a conscience effort to name Belshazzar's father and grandfather because they were both strong kings, but Belshazzar was a weakling and there is no glory in conquering a weak opponent. Hence, all their accounts leave him out.

The Greeks got their history from the Persians and Herodotus and Xenophon also leave out the name of Belshazzar. Herodotus did get it right about the time and means of how Babylon fell however, and the details match perfectly with the account in Daniel 6. It wasn't until archeologists found Babylonian inscriptions such as the Cylinder of Nebuchadnezzar, the Nabonidus Chronicle and the Verse Account of Nabonidus and other Babylonia texts that there were secular accounts that matched the details in Daniel 6. In other words, for some who even call themselves Christians, it is easier to believe secular "experts", than the Word of God. But those who are wise believe God's Word is exactly that and is therefore true!

60

THE SECRETS OF ARCHIMEDES

"The secret things belong to the LORD our God, but the things revealed belong to us and to our sons forever, that we may observe all the words of this law."

DEUTERONOMY 29:29

I would be remiss to not have a reflection on what I consider the greatest Greek of all—Archimedes. Most of us have heard about the famous Greek polymath Archimedes (287–212 BC). Probably the greatest scientist of the ancient world, he was an expert in the field of mathematics, physics, engineering, and astronomy, to name just a few subjects. His most famous story is how he discovered what is known as "Archimedes Principle" which shows that different objects make up different volumes. In brief, any object that is immersed in fluid is acted upon by an upward/buoyant force that is equal to the weight of the fluid displaced by the object. It is said that when he stepped into a tub full of water, he noticed the water rose. This was an observation which solved a problem he was working on and he was so excited about the solution he ran into the streets of the city of Syracuse naked yelling "Eureka," which means "I found it."

He was also famous for the application of his equations and formulas for inventing things, but unfortunately nothing of his was written down, so everything was lost. That is until in 1906, a 174-page document known as the "Archimedes Palimpsest" was discovered at a monastery. Before paper was used in the western world, animal skins known as "parchment" was used for writing material. Because animal skins were expensive, often old writings were scrapped off and then written over for another writing project. There is a long history of this document and how it came to the monastery, but a researcher was reading the document and noticed there was some faint, older writing underneath the main text. Further study on the original writing showed it was a sixth-century AD author who was using Archimedes's original studies on geometry and other mathematical proofs.

What was once considered lost for all time, was something that showed how Archimedes came upon some of his greatest discoveries and ideas. In the same light, the verse above shows that God Himself knows all the secrets, and we will never know the full extent of His glory, power and secrets of the universe. However, there are some things that we can discover because as He reveals Himself to us, we learn more about Him. The wonder and depths of the richness of God and the created order, are for us to learn one day at a time for of all time.

APPENDIX

ABBREVIATED GREEK HISTORY TIMELINE

ARCHAIC PERIOD (785–481 BC)

776 BC Traditional date for the first historic Olympic games.

Late 8th to early 7th century BC, Homer writes *Iliad* and *Odyssey.*

621 BC Draco, Athenian lawgiver, issues code of laws, with many crimes punishable by death.

513 BC Persia annexes Thrace (Region).

490 BC Themistocles, Miltiades, and Athenians, defeat Darius at Marathon, Phidippides runs with news.

484 BC Aeschylus, Athenian playwright wins his first victory at the City of Dionysia.

480 BC Leonidas, Spartan, sacrifices 300 Spartan soldiers at the Battle of Thermopylae so main force can escape; Xerxes son of Darius is commanding the Persians.

480 BC Simultaneous with Battle of Thermopylae, the Greeks and Persians fight to a draw in the naval Battle of Artemisium.

480 BC Battle of Salamis; Themistocles, Athenian general, lures Persians into Bay of Salamis, of Xerxes loses and goes home, leaving behind Mardonius.

479 BC Pausanias, Greek general routs Mardonius at the Battle of Plataea.

478 BC Delian League is founded by Athens.

474 BC Pindar, Greek poet relocates to Thebes (in Greece) from court at Syracuse.

471 BC Themistocles is ostracized.

460 BC First Peloponnesian War starts (460–445)

457 BC Pericles, Athenian statesman begins Golden Age; he was taught by Anaxagora, by who believed in dualistic Universe and atoms.

451 BC Sparta commanded by King Achidamus II prepares to destroy Athens, thus starting the Peloponnesian War.

449 BC Herodotus, Greek historian, begins to writes history of the Greco-Persian War (490–479 BC).

447 BC Parthenon construction begins in Athens.

445 BC First Peloponnesian War ends.

435 BC Phidias, Greek sculptor, completes statue of Zeus at Elis, 1 of 7 wonders of the world.

432 BC End of "Golden Age" of Athens.

431 BC Empedocles, Greek doctor, believes body has Four Temperaments.

430 BC Failed peace mission by Athens, bubonic plague year, Sparta takes no prisoners.

429 BC Pericles dies of Athenian Plague, possibly typhus or bubonic plague.

429 BC Hippocates, Greek doctor, believes diseases have physical cause.

428 BC Plato is born.

421 BC Peace of Nicias brings temporary end to war, but Alcibiades, a nephew of Pericles, makes anti-Sparta alliance.

415–413 BC Siege of Syracuse results in Roman victory and control of Sicily.

414 BC Lamachus, Athenian commander killed at Syracuse.

413 BC Nicias and Demosthenes are killed at Syracuse.

411 BC Sparta allies with Persia.

405 BC Naval Battle of Aegospotami and Spartan fleet destroys Athenian navy.

c. 402–318 BC Phocion, Athenian statesman and general brings reform to Athens.

401 BC Thucydides, Greek historian, leaves account of "Golden Age of Pericles" and Peloponnesian War at his death (History of the Peloponnesian War).

399 BC Socrates, Greek philosopher, condemned to death for corrupting youth.

c. 380–370 BC Plato writes *The Republic.*

c. 370 BC Xenophon writes *Anabasis.*

347 BC Plato, Greek philosopher, founder of the Academy, dies.

342 BC Aristotle, Greek philosopher, begins teaching Alexander, son of Philip of Macedon.

336 BC Alexander succeeds father Philip II, who was assassinated by Pausanias of Orestis.

333 BC Alexander defeats Persians at Battle of Issus, but Darius III escapes.

332 BC Alexander conquers Egypt.

332 BC Alexandria is founded by Alexander the Great.

331 BC At the Battle of Gaugamela, October 1, Alexander ends Achaemenid Dynasty and conquers Persian Empire.

331 BC Alexander the Great enters Babylon

327 BC Alexander invades northern India, but his army is despondent and refuses to march further eastwards.

HELLENISTIC GREECE (323–30 BC)

323 BC Alexander dies, his generals vie for power in Wars of the Diadochi.

323–322 BC Lamian War or Hellenic War ensues in unsuccessful attempt by Athens to end Macedonian hegemony.

322–281 BC Wars of Succession (also known as Wars of the Diadochi) are fought by generals of Alexander the Great to determine who will succeed him in ruling his empire.

319–272 BC Pyrrhus of Epirus

312–63 BC Seleucid Empire controls western Asia after Alexander's death.

305–30 BC Ptolemaic Kingdom controls ancient Egypt as Egypt's longest-lasting dynasty.

300 BC Euclid, Greek mathematician, publishes *Elements,* treating both geometry and number theory.

287–212 BC Archimedes, Greek mathematician, develops Archimedes' screw, specific gravity concept, center of gravity concept, concepts of buoyancy and volume, and anticipates discoveries of integral calculus.

280 BC Battle of Heraclea results in Greek victory over Romans but with severe losses.

280–275 BC Pyrric War is won by the Roman Republic.

279 BC Battle of Asculum is fought and there is minimal documentation of the conflict and different versions of the victor.

88 BC City of Athens is sacked by Roman forces

30 BC Death of Ptolemaic Queen Cleopatra, last ruler of the Ptolemaic Kingdom occurs.

RECOMMENDED READING

Any person desiring to read and learn more about the history of Greece has a lifetime's worth of primary and secondary sources available to him or her. Listed below are a few titles that have been especially helpful and enjoyable to the author.

Aristotle, *Aristotle's Politics,* second ed. Carnes Lord, trans and ed. Chicago: University of Chicago Press, 2013.

Boardman, John, Jasper Griffin, and Oswyn Murray, eds. *The Oxford History of Greece & the Hellenistic World.* 2nd ed. New York: Oxford University Press, 2002.

Grant, Michael, ed. *Greek Literature: An Anthology–Translations from Greek Prose and Poetry.* New York: Penguin Classics, 1977.

Homer. *The Iliad,* Emily Wilson, trans. New York: W. W. Norton & Co., 2023.

________. *The Odyssey,* Emily Wilson, trans. New York: W. W. Norton & Co., 2017.

Kagan, Donald. *The Peloponnesian War.* New York: Viking, 2003.

Kagan, Donald and Gregory F. Viffiano, eds. *Men of Bronze: Hoplite Warfare in Ancient Greece.* Reprint ed. Princeton, NJ: Princeton University Press, 2015.

Lendon, J. E. *Soldiers and Ghosts: A History of Battles in Classical Antiquity.* New Haven: Yale University Press, 2005.

Markos, Louis. *Ancient Voices: An Insider's Look at Classical Greece.* Middletown, RI: Stone Tower Press, 2020.

________. *From Achilles to Christ: Why Christians Should Read the Pagan Classics.* Downers Grove: IVP Academic, 2007.

________. *Worldview Guide for The Iliad.* Moscow, ID: Canon Press, 2017.

________. *Worldview Guide for The Odyssey.* Moscow, ID: Canon Press, 2017.

Plato. *The Republic.* Allan Boom, trans. New York: Basic Books, 2016.

Strassler, Robert B., ed., et al. *The Landmark Herodotus: The Histories.* New York: Pantheon Books, 2007.

Strassler, Robert B. ed and Richard Crawley, trans. *The Landmark Thucydides: A Comprehensive Guide to the Peloponnesian War.* New York: Free Pres, 1998.

Strassler, Robert B., ed. *The Landmark Xenophon's Hellenika.* New York: Pantheon Books, 2009.

Strauss, Barry. *The Battle of Salamis: The Naval Encounter That Saved Greece–and Western Civilization.* New York: Simon & Shuster, 2004.

ABOUT THE AUTHOR

Robert Freiberg (M.Div., Th.M., D.Min., D.D.) is currently an adjunct professor at Central Baptist Theological Seminary in Minneapolis for chaplain ministries. As a 27-year Navy chaplain, now retired, he wrote a daily "Morning Blessings" devotional that went out to every computer at every command in which he served. From the Navy SEALs Headquarters (NAVSPECWARCEN, WARCOM) to an aircraft carrier at sea (USS *Carl Vinson* CVN-70) to the Marine Aviation Wing (3MAW) in Iraq, hundreds of thousands of Navy and Marine Corps personnel received (with command permission) practical biblical advice and daily encouragement given through the lessons of ancient history. He is still producing these daily for anyone who would like to read them (bob@morningblessings.org).

Dr. Freiberg has also served as Dean of Administration and taught Theology and Church History at Southern California Seminary in El Cajon, California, as well as currently teaching military and institutional chaplaincy ministry to Zambian military and fire, police, and hospital chaplains. He is a board member of the Associated Gospel Churches (AGC) and serves as the editor for the *AGC Journal,* a semi-annual professional journal for chaplains, pastors, seminary professors and others interested in furthering the gospel of Christ (AGCJournal.com). He is a regular contributor for this publication, specializing in the Christian beginnings of the Colonial and Revolutionary War era.

Bob lives with his wife of 48 years, Nancy. Their son John is a missionary planting churches in Asian countries. When Bob and Nancy are not traveling, Bob's enjoys working in his Roman Garden, where the floor plans were taken from a Roman villa and replicated in his backyard.